Prais
Leaning int

'In a thoughtful and pragmatic way, Binney and Williams importantly describe the multifaceted organizational learning and leadership agendas required of successful change efforts. Clearly a book that is at home on my top shelf, together with the likes of Senge's *Fifth Discipline* and Hamel/Prahalad's *Competing for the Future.*'
Howard Selland, President, Aeroquip Corporation

'Binney and Williams achieve their ambitious goal of recognising the full complexity of change and providing some practical guidance on how to manage the process...solidly and vividly grounded in considerable experience of change management.'
David Arnold, Harvard Business School

'I like the insistence that CEOs have to do apparently opposite things, which is certainly a world I recognize. I also like the style of writing and the more reflective, semi-psychological approach.'
Chris Hogg, Chairman, Courtaulds plc

'This book provides both helpful insights and practical ideas for managers leading change in organizations.'
Pierre Bilger, Chief Executive Officer, GEC ALSTHOM

'A breath of fresh air. It approaches many of the current managerial fads with a healthy scepticism but recognises the kernels of value where they exist. Binney and Williams take these valued elements and have constructed a model of change which combines top down and bottom up change processes.

'In so doing they have arrived at a synergy which is immensely powerful and provides corrective, practical guidance to the many busy executives who have started down this route and wonder why they have not succeeded. Those who have not yet begun will save themselves much time and effort by reading and heeding *Leaning into the Future.*'
Professor Peter D Wickens OBE

'This book goes to the core of running a successful business…a salutary reminder that context is all important. For those who want to deal with the messy realities of business today, it's a very powerful insight.

'The book has helped me enormously. It shows the danger of pushing harder and harder at the change programmes and failing to see the wood for the trees. Too many managers are doing for the sake of being seen to be doing. They are not keeping in balance the need to stop and think. Sometimes they should 'lean into the future' more before starting to run.'

David Etherington, Head of Corporate Business Development,
National Westminster Bank

'The insurance industry, in common with most others, is in a period of intense radical change. I am sure that any manager engaged in this will relate to the ideas in this book and find them stimulating.'

Allan Bridgewater, Chief Executive,
Norwich Union Insurance Group

Leaning into
the Future

Leaning into the Future

Future

Changing the way people change organisations

George Binney &
Colin Williams

NICHOLAS BREALEY
PUBLISHING

LONDON

This paperback edition first published by
Nicholas Brealey Publishing Limited in 1997

First published in hardback by
Nicholas Brealey Publishing Limited in 1995

36 John Street
London
WC1N 2AT, UK
Tel: +44 (0)171 430 0224
Fax: +44 (0)171 404 8311

17470 Sonoma Highway
Sonoma
California 95476, USA
Tel: (707) 939 7570
Fax: (707) 938 3515

Reprinted 1996 (twice)

ISBN 1-85788-083-8

British Library Cataloguing in Publication Data
A catalogue record for this book is available from the British Library.

Printed and bound in Great Britain by
Biddles Ltd, Guildford and King's Lynn

Contents

Preface   ix

Chapter 1   Leaning into the future   1

Chapter 2   The myth of managing change   11

Chapter 3   Flawed assumptions about change   31

Chapter 4   Forthright *and* listening leadership   54

Chapter 5   Seeing clearly   78

Chapter 6   Working with the grain   102

Chapter 7   All change!   121

Chapter 8   Learning while doing   138

Chapter 9   The dynamic interplay of 'opposites'   157

References   169

Index   173

To Deborah and Sarah
To Odile, Daphné, Marion and Nicolas

Preface

Over the years of working with and studying different organisations, we have been influenced by many individuals. We want to record our gratitude here to all of them, while recognising that sometimes it is difficult months or years after discussions to disentangle who contributed what and how.

We are particularly grateful to our colleagues at Ashridge who have been extraordinarily generous with their support and insights. We think especially of Bill Critchley, Alex Knight, Robin Ladkin and Hugh Pidgeon who have all contributed important ideas and/or commented on earlier drafts of the book. Andrea Jackman has been consistently enthusiastic and effective in her marshalling of the material and of us.

Outside Ashridge, Bonnie Dean of Aeroquip, Gerry O'Hagen of IDV and Ariane Berthoin Antal of Wissenschaftszentrum, Berlin provided valuable, detailed feedback on drafts of the book. Gerhard Wilke contributed important ideas and encouragement and worked on the health service project featured in Chapter 5 and elsewhere in the book.

Nicholas Brealey has been a remarkable publisher: incisive, encouraging and patient. We have gained much from working with him and with our editor, Sally Yeung.

But our best thanks go to all the individual managers and client organisations with whom we have worked on issues of strategic change over the last 10 years. Over countless meetings, workshops, informal discussions and other work together, they have shaped our thinking. We are very grateful for the opportunity to work with them and the permission to quote here some of their stories.

They include businesses in many different types of industry and situation: companies that have been highly successful which now face abrupt changes in their environments (for example, Norwich Union), organisations which are being privatised (British Rail), companies which have come back from the brink of disaster (Courtaulds) but continue to face severe international competition, and companies which have recovered after poor performance (Kleinwort Benson). They also include 'greenfield' enterprises (National Westminster Life Assurance), large companies (Milliken) and smaller or medium-sized ones (HP Bulmer). We have worked with organisations which are established under a variety of public sector regimes (the European Patent Office and GP practices in south-east England) and experienced issues from the corporate (GEC ALSTHOM and BSG International) and from the operating company perspective (J&B Scotland, Booker Farming and Aeroquip's European Industrial Division). Examples and stories from these organisations are presented throughout the book.

The second source of inspiration comes from our research work. In 1991 and 1992, in association with The Economist, we undertook a major research project to look at the efforts to bring about change under the banner of total quality. The results of this research were published by The Economist Intelligence Unit: *Making Quality Work – Lessons from Europe's Leading Companies*. In total 46 companies were involved, of which six became in-depth case studies: a French-based international company (Club Med), a Danish-owned international group (Grundfos), an Italian company (Ciba-Geigy's operation in that country), a Japanese company (Nissan) and an American enterprise (Federal Express) operating in the UK and a UK multinational (ICL).

A decade of work with, and researching, organisations in change has raised many questions about how companies and organisations handle change. We have seen directors, managers and staff all working like crazy to 'bring about' change. Usually the reasons for change are compelling and the intentions are honest. Yet often there is a sense of frustration and waste. Waste of energy, waste of time, waste of money and people's emotions – too much pain, too much suffering, too much disappointment.

We offer a different way: a way of working with change that leaves people feeling better about themselves and about others and achieves more of what they want. That is what we set out in the following chapters.

1

Leaning into the future

'Leaning into the future' is a way of thinking about and working with change. It is the way we make sense of our experience in the last decade with over 100 organisations, identifying why some individuals work successfully with radical organisational change while others are frustrated and exhausted.

Many people are battling with far-reaching organisational change. Banks and insurance companies, for example, are trying to become more responsive to customers and faster on their feet in adapting to changing markets and regulation. Manufacturing companies are seeking to cope with the awesome pressures of increasingly global competition, to develop the right new products and services at the same time as increasing quality and dramatically reducing costs. Health services are caught in a whirlwind of change, under pressure to be more managerial and cost conscious while coping with ever-increasing patient expectations. Professional partnerships are often facing severe competition, increasingly volatile markets and pressures to become bigger and offer a wider range of services. Companies are being privatised throughout the developed world and old certainties swept away in the drive for cost reduction and profit. Government is not immune: administration is giving way to management, safety and security to value for money and the effort to be more responsive to the citizen.

Very often managers have put in place some form of 'top-down' change programme in order to achieve these changes: sometimes under the banner of 'business process reengineering', sometimes 'total quality management' or 'continuous improvement', in other organisations 'vision and values', 'culture change', 'reforms', or simply 'reorganisation' or 'turnaround'. Although the names differ, the key elements of vision-led change, driven from the top, working through structured programmes, are the same. The key is assertive leadership, clear about where it wants organisations to go and determined to reach there.

Less common in practice, but well developed in theory, have been efforts to handle change through a 'bottom-up', 'self-directing' approach, derived from an understanding of organisations as living systems. This challenges structured, 'top-down' change head on. It suggests that organisational change cannot be managed: it evolves and cannot be made the subject of plans and programmes. The job of managers should be to 'allow' organisations to adjust to change, to remove the blocks that prevent individuals realising their potential to develop and grow. In this view the key is learning, the capacity to respond and adjust in the face of changing circumstances and environments.

In this book we question both the 'top-down' change programmes and the 'bottom-up' approach – not because they are wrong but because they are incomplete. In their different ways both leave out key elements. Successful leaders of change are reaching beyond these approaches to a more rewarding way of working with change.

The 'top-down' change programmes have certain common features:

Top-down change programmes

❖ Leader as hero

❖ Vision

❖ Drive

❖ 'They' are the problem

❖ Training

All emphasise the importance of decisive inspirational leadership: top managers who know what the answer is and will others to follow. They see vision as the source of energy for change: identifying and communicating a persuasive picture of the future organisation they want to build. The programmes assume that change must be driven through: people, it is said, are naturally conservative. Left to themselves they will resist change or refuse to change fast enough. They also assume that radical change can be planned and programmed: the orderly application of force will overcome the 'resistance' to change that is said to exist in organisations.

These change programmes work from an assumption that 'they' are the problem. Who 'they' are depends on the individual's perspective: from the point of view of senior management it is middle managers or front-line workers. Finally, change programmes involve extensive training efforts. It is assumed that people can be taught new ways of working: explain the principles, provide new tools and techniques and, hey presto, people will change the way they operate.

'Top-down' change programmes often do not work. They do not produce the intended effects; instead of transforming organisations, they produce mediocre results. Very often these programmes are short-term fixes, achieving necessary changes such as cost reduction, but not shifting corporate cultures in the way that is needed for sustainable success.

Many change programmes leave people feeling frustrated and exhausted. As consultants we see inside many different organisations and have access to people at all levels, who speak (relatively) freely about what they think and feel. Frequently we see managers and staff expressing how battered they feel by endless change initiatives. Often managers preface these views by some formal comments such as: 'it's doing fine, perhaps a little behind schedule', or 'patchy but overall OK'. But when people begin to relax, a different story emerges. Because programmes assume that change must be 'done to' organisations, people often have a sense of being imposed on, of not being valued or respected. They become angry and cynical, less rather than more likely to give of their best for the organisation.

People frequently live in a state of constant insecurity, worrying about where the next reorganisation or redundancy will leave them. Their energies become consumed in defending what they have, rather than considering what they can create together with other people in the company. Often there is a pattern of anxious activity – more meetings, more working groups and taskforces, more new initiatives – but little sense that the organisation is tackling the root causes of its difficulties.

So these change programmes are at best a partial answer – at worst they damage the capacity of organisations to respond to change in the future. For us they are not the way forward.

But equally we question the zealous application of the view of organisations as 'living systems' and the 'bottom-up', self-organizing approach to change which it has spawned. This approach has the following features:

Bottom-up approach

❖ Leader as facilitator

❖ Awareness

❖ Release

❖ 'We' need to change

❖ Reflection

According to this view change is all around us, all the time: it should not be seen as deeply disturbing. Managers need not feel under relentless pressure to 'make change happen': instead their job is to facilitate, to enable others to realise more of their potential. Managers need to work at becoming more aware of current realities and of the change that happens naturally without anyone causing it to happen. They should consider what they can do to release the natural capacity of individuals to develop: not making learning happen but reducing the blocks which organisations and managers put in the way of learning.

This view argues that change in the nature of organisations cannot be 'managed' at all: it cannot be planned and predicted, made the subject of a 14-step programme. The unexpected always occurs and unintended consequences have an unhappy habit of displacing the intended ones. Cause and effect are not linear: if a manager does 'A', it is not possible to say whether 'B' will follow: there are too many interconnections and interdependencies. Instead of constantly 'doing', individuals should step back more often and reflect on the underlying causes of difficulties and the choices open to them.

In the 'living systems' picture, change in the nature of organisations becomes a process of exploration, in which leaders as well as followers are learning.

However, just as 'top-down' programmes have not delivered the expected results, so too have 'bottom-up' efforts led to frustration. As one director said to us: 'We've tried hard to empower and to involve, but ultimately people have ended up going round in circles. We've not made progress in dealing with the key business issues. We've had lots of activity but it has been unfocused. It hasn't addressed the key problems we have as a business.'

Sometimes efforts to involve and 'empower' have led to what one of our clients calls the 'stationery cupboard' phenomenon: people spending hours working out how to deal with trivial issues while much more important problems go unanswered.

Or they lead to inaction: staff told suddenly to use their initiative, who did not ask to be 'empowered' and are frightened by the responsibility they have been given. They can become frozen, unclear what boundaries they are working within and unable to contribute anything effective.

Thus those who want to lead change face a difficulty. Neither 'top-down' change programmes nor the 'self-organising', 'bottom-up' approach are wholly convincing. Yet there is a need to do something. The pressures to change – to improve quality, cut costs, develop service, change the culture – are more insistent than ever.

Leading *and* learning = leaning into the future

In this book we offer a different view of organisational change and of what individuals can do. Our experience is that successful leaders of change do not adopt either the 'top-down' or the 'bottom-up' view: they build on the strengths of *both* approaches and work in a way that combines their insights and embraces the contradictions and tensions between them.

Central to 'top-down' change programmes is the emphasis on *leading* change, the realisation that if people just let change happen, they are unlikely to achieve the results they want. Every successful change process we have seen has involved individuals who are clear about what they do and don't want and determined to achieve as much of this as possible. And if individuals are to lead, they need to focus attention on particular priorities through campaigns or programmes.

Central to the 'bottom-up' approach is the realisation that processes of radical change involve *learning* for everyone involved, including those who seek to lead. What is characteristic of the transformations which people are seeking is that they require radical shifts in thinking as well as behaviour. In the famous words of Einstein: 'The problems we face cannot be resolved at the same level of thinking as that which gave rise to them.' Everyone has to learn, including leaders.

Successful leaders in change combine leading *and* learning: they lead in such a way that learning is encouraged; they learn in a way that informs and guides those who seek to lead. This is what we call *leaning into the future*.

These leaders combine clear direction with creating space for others to take initiative: they are straight talking, forthright and yet highly effective listeners. In their hands providing direction and allowing autonomy, being forthright and listening are not contradictory: they are complementary. Again and again we have been struck by how the apparent opposites interact and reinforce one another. Success in handling one objective enables the apparently opposite aim also to be managed successfully.

Thus the forthright *and* listening leadership we describe has a gutsy, uncompromising, personal risk-taking feel which is more than the simple exertion of willpower: more than 'do it because I've told you to do it'. And it has an element of genuinely listening and responding to others' wants and needs which goes beyond conventional good management. The elements of assertive leadership and responsiveness reinforce one another: because individuals are being themselves, sticking out for the things they really believe, they have more capacity to attend to others. By setting clear objectives and standards, they offer the boundaries within which it is possible for others to exercise autonomy.

Critical is the way these leaders provide direction and are forthright. They do both very assertively, but they leave room for the contribution of others and they are genuinely responsive. They encourage other people to take the initiative and to state their views clearly.

By combining leading *and* learning in this way individuals make possible the other features of 'leaning into the future'.

They develop 'seeing clearly', a genuine shared understanding of current reality, not visions and wish lists, to provide the energy for change. They develop from existing strengths, identifying rigorously what the organisation does well and what it needs to develop.

They 'work with the grain', shaping change with clear intentions but doing so with respect for the context and substance, as does a sculptor or wood carver. They plan ahead in order to be better prepared when the unpredictable happens. Paradoxically, by recognising the limits of what they can do, they become more effective. They don't challenge the impossible but focus their energies where they can succeed.

They recognise that leadership in change is everyone's responsibility and something that requires people to look deep into themselves before addressing others' faults. They foster leading by people of all types and all levels in organisations, not just top managers. They work with people as they are, attending to their feelings and emotions as well as logic and facts.

Finally, they know the importance of 'learning while doing', reflecting and learning in the context of real-life priorities and tasks, not classroom exercises. They look at best practice in other organisations in order to understand themselves better.

Thus the leaders we describe in this book have not chosen either 'top-down' programmes or the 'bottom-up' approach, nor have they 'mixed and matched' the approaches, taking a little bit of one and a little bit of the other. They have reframed the issue of working with change and reached *beyond* these alternatives. They have rethought the business of organisational change. For them what may appear opposite aims are in fact complementary. What others may see as a paradox – how can an individual be both assertive and listening? – they see as two sides of the same coin.

They are not perturbed by the tension between leading and learning but work with it and exploit it. Just as a sailor tacking into the wind steers first one way, then another, in order to reach their objective, so individuals who handle change effectively steer a winding course between leading and learning, first emphasising one objective, then the other. They do so in such a way that their success in leading encourages learning and their effectiveness in learning fosters leading. How they achieve this outstanding combination is the subject of this book.

THE STRUCTURE OF THE BOOK

In Chapter 2 we describe the characteristics of 'top-down' change programmes and the real-life difficulties managers have encountered with them. Then in Chapter 3 we look at the assumptions that underlie these change programmes and why they represent a mechanical picture of organisations; we also examine the alternative 'bottom-up' approach inspired by viewing organisations as living systems. This enables us to identify the strengths of the two alternative views and show how 'leaning into the future' goes beyond them.

In the following chapters we explore what 'leaning into the future' means for individuals. Chapter 4 deals with the type of leadership involved: forthright and listening, clear about what it wants and responsive to those around it. In Chapter 5 we examine 'seeing clearly': how, paradoxically, the energy for change comes not from ringing declarations of intent but from greater awareness of the present and past and the possibilities that are available. Chapter 6 describes how people can 'work with the grain' of change in their organisations, releasing some of the untapped desire to improve and develop.

Chapter 7 deals with 'all change', the recognition that everyone has responsibility for change and that leaders need to look deep into themselves if they are to provide an effective lead to others. Chapter 8 is concerned with 'learning while doing', shifting thinking and behaviour in the course of dealing with current tasks and priorities.

Finally, in Chapter 9 we summarise the approach and its implications for managers.

LEANING INTO THE FUTURE = AND

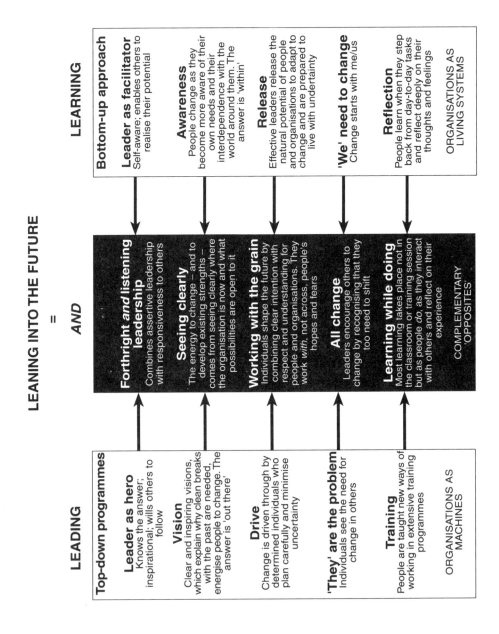

LEARNING

Bottom-up approach

Leader as facilitator
Self-aware; enables others to realise their potential

Awareness
People change as they become more aware of their own needs and their interdependence with the world around them. The answer is 'within'

Release
Effective leaders release the natural potential of people and organisations to adapt to change and are prepared to live with uncertainty

'We' need to change
Change starts with me/us

Reflection
People learn when they step back from day-to-day tasks and reflect deeply on their thoughts and feelings

ORGANISATIONS AS LIVING SYSTEMS

Forthright *and* listening leadership
Combines assertive leadership with responsiveness to others

Seeing clearly
The energy to change – and to develop existing strengths – comes from seeing clearly where the organisation is now and what possibilities are open to it

Working with the grain
Individuals shape the future by combining clear intention with respect and understanding for people and organisations. They work *with*, not across, people's hopes and fears

All change
Leaders encourage others to change by recognising that they too need to shift

Learning while doing
Most learning takes place not in the classroom or training session but as people *do*, as they interact with others and reflect on their experience

COMPLEMENTARY 'OPPOSITES'

LEADING

Top-down programmes

Leader as hero
Knows the answer; inspirational; wills others to follow

Vision
Clear and inspiring visions, which explain why clean breaks with the past are needed, energise people to change. The answer is 'out there'

Drive
Change is driven through by determined individuals who plan carefully and minimise uncertainty

'They' are the problem
Individuals see the need for change in others

Training
People are taught new ways of working in extensive training programmes

ORGANISATIONS AS MACHINES

© George Binney and Colin Williams

2

The Myth of Managing Change

'Managing change!' The phrase rings out like a clarion call across organisations far and wide. It sounds like the secret of success, the elixir which will enable managers to steer their organisations to survival and growth. It is a tantalising proposition. What a weight would be taken off the minds of leaders if they could discover the formula, understand the recipe and create this magic.

Many different organisations have sought to transform some aspect of the way they work in order to adapt when circumstances change. They have wanted to change the 'code' of their organisations: the often unwritten rules that govern how people behave.

NatWest Life, for example, like many banks and insurance companies in the last 10 years, has sought to make the transition from bureaucracy to service-led organisation. And like those in many other organisations, managers at NatWest Life have recognised that this is not a trivial matter. A revolution in attitudes, systems and structures has been necessary to begin to make this transition. A revolution, for example, in the way front-line staff go about their jobs: no longer just achieving certain output levels and applying the rules, but also now feeling responsible and capable of improving the way the work is done.

Or take a smaller organisation. Doctors, nurses and staff operating in primary care teams have faced a whirlwind of change in the last six to seven years. One of the changes is that instead of caring only for the sick they are now expected to work for health promotion, to encourage their patients to lead healthier lives. Such a change goes to the heart of a doctor's practice. It doesn't just affect ways of working; it also requires the relationships between doctors and nurses, medical staff and others to change and challenges the basis of doctors' professional self-esteem. The role of a doctor in encouraging patients to give up smoking or take regular exercise is a lot less mysterious and skilled than the job of diagnosing and treating illness. Some doctors fear that they are being pushed to become the educational agents of central government rather then independent professionals.

What is characteristic of these transformations is that they involve a radical shift in thinking as well as behaviour. Underlying the patterns of behaviour that define organisations are the mental models that people have, the assumptions and frameworks that enable them to make sense of the world. For example, does a company exist to make money, to exploit a technology or expertise, to serve customers, to have fun? Or a mix of these and other purposes? What beliefs do people have about 'what business are we in?', 'what does it take to succeed in this business?', 'what sort of people do we need?', 'how do you manage people to get results?'

It is these mental models or paradigms that ultimately organisations have sought to change. And that, of course, is why change is often difficult. It is very difficult to let go of these mental models. To give them up is to let go of part of ourselves, part of our identity, the part that allows us to understand the world and stops it being a terrifying mass of confusion. Again and again people in organisations have held on to patterns of thinking and behaviour long after the world that gave rise to them has changed. Twenty years ago Andrew Pettigrew showed how companies often hold on to flagrantly faulty assumptions about their world for as long as a decade, despite overwhelming evidence that the world has changed. But how can you bring about this change in mental models? How can individuals help their company or organisation adapt to changing circumstances?

THE CHARACTERISTICS OF CHANGE PROGRAMMES

The most commonly used approach in recent years has been some form of 'top-down' change programme. There are many varieties of this, but all have five key characteristics in common:

❖ vision
❖ telling people what that vision is
❖ top management determination
❖ planning and programming
❖ adopting best practice

One of many exponents of this approach – and one whom we respect very much – is John Kotter of Harvard Business School. He explains why change programmes put vision at centre stage:

In every successful transformation effort that I have seen, the guiding coalition develops a picture of the future that is relatively easy to communicate and appeals to customers, stockholders, and employees... In failed transformations, on the other hand, you find plenty of plans and directives and programs, but no vision... A vision goes beyond the numbers that are typically found in five-year plans... It says something that helps clarify the direction in which an organization needs to move.

What is needed is to knit together the change efforts in different parts of an organisation and to motivate participants in the change efforts. Kotter suggests a rule of thumb: 'If you can't communicate the vision to someone in five minutes or less and get a reaction that signifies both understanding and interest, you are not done with this phase of the transformation process.'

Whose vision is this? Generally that of the person at the top of the organisation, sometimes that of a small group of senior managers. That's the job of a chief executive: to create and communicate the vision of the future of the organisation.

Once developed, the vision has to be communicated effectively. Top managers must tell people what future they are trying to create. Kotter puts the case:

> *Transformation is impossible unless hundreds or thousands of people are willing to help, often to the point of making short term sacrifices. Employees will not make sacrifices, even if they are unhappy with the status quo, unless they believe useful change is possible. Without credible communication, and a lot of it, the hearts and minds of the troops are never captured.*

That's the phrase that crops up again and again in change programmes: 'hearts and minds'. The task is to win them and the means are to market, to sell the vision, to persuade. Kotter continues: 'In successful transformation efforts, executives use all existing communication channels to broadcast the vision.'

They probably also create new channels to get the message across. It is recognised that executives who communicate well incorporate messages into their hour-by-hour activities and in the famous phrase that they must 'walk the talk', consciously seeking to become living symbols of the new corporate culture. 'Communication comes in both words and deeds and the latter are often the most powerful form,' says Kotter.

In communicating the vision another characteristic of change management thinking becomes apparent: determination and drive. According to Lord Weinstock, chief executive of GEC, in successful change 'there is only one factor and it is *will*', the absolute determination to bring about the change that is required. As Sir Allen Sheppard of Grand Metropolitan has put it:

> *Self-generated strategic change requires the stamina, the endurance and the resilience to just keep coming back to that strategy. You get knocked partly off, but you come back again. You get knocked the other way off, but you come back. You're not going to arrive if you get diverted.*

One reason sheer willpower is so important is that there are likely to be many in every organisation who will, it is said, 'resist change'. The change management literature abounds with discussion of the possible causes of resistance and how to overcome them. According to Tony Eccles in *Succeeding with Change*: 'The pressures for change in an organization have to contend with forces of inertia that will resist any significant displacement of the status quo.' Those ready to resist will include those who want the organisation to change, but not in the direction that has been chosen. They may also be fearful. As Lord Weinstock has said: 'Almost by definition you have found fault and want to make things better. If you want to change, then there must be some people faults – so they are fearful.'

Change in recent years has, of course, often entailed reductions in employee numbers, closures, redundancies, loss of position and loss of benefits. So it's not surprising that groups are seen as 'resistors of change'. In the sights are often middle managers, sometimes front-line staff, sometimes senior managers who are said to be fearful of change and slow to shift in the ways the organisation requires: different people make different assessments of where the blockages lie.

To overcome resistance careful planning and preparation are needed. Change programme approaches may vary, but they all contain this emphasis on thinking through what change you want to bring about and preparing implementation in a logical, sequential way. John Kotter proposes 'Eight Steps to Transforming Your Organization' (see Figure 2.1).

① **Establishing a sense of urgency**

Examining market and competitive realities
Identifying and discussing crises, potential crises or major opportunities

② **Forming a powerful guiding coalition**

Assembling a group with enough power to lead the change effort
Encouraging the group to work together as a team

③ **Creating a vision**

Creating a vision to help direct the change effort
Developing strategies for achieving that vision

④ **Communicating the vision**

Using every vehicle possible to communicate the new vision and
strategies
Teaching new behaviors by the example of the guiding coalition

⑤ **Empowering others to act on the vision**

Getting rid of obstacles to change
Changing systems or structures that seriously undermine the vision
Encouraging risk taking and nontraditional ideas, activities, and actions

⑥ **Planning for and creating short-term wins**

Planning for viable performance improvements
Creating those improvements
Recognizing and rewarding employees involved in the improvements

⑦ **Consolidating improvements and producing still more change**

Using increased credibility to change systems, structures, and policies
that don't fit the vision
Hiring, promoting, and developing employees who can implement the
vision
Reinvigorating the process with new projects, themes, and change
agents

⑧ **Institutionalizing new approaches**

Articulating the connections between the new behaviors and corporate
success
Developing the means to ensure leadership development and
succession

*Figure 2.1   Eight Steps to Transforming Your Organization
(Kotter, 1995)*

Often the planning centres on 'gap analysis': measuring the gap between where the organisation is now and the vision and then planning how to fill it. To oversee and coordinate the necessary steps, the advocates of change programmes typically recommend that a steering group is formed. This is a group of senior managers and others eager for change which has the responsibility of ensuring that the steps are made in the correct sequence, that the organisation does not rush to the later stages of change before the early ones are complete; also that change processes and actions are 'aligned', that is consistent one with another. Has the vision, for example, been well enough communicated for everyone to understand it and be willing to act on it? Does the style of management and leadership practised in the organisation support the vision?

The team has to consider the 'obstacles' to change and how to overcome or avoid them. Perhaps overly narrow job descriptions prevent staff thinking about improvement or customers. Reward and incentive schemes may cause people to think about selfish and departmental concerns in preference to corporate interests. Or perhaps key individuals are only paying lip-service to the need for change and must be persuaded to give genuine support or be moved to another part of the organisation.

Also important is applying best practice from other organisations. There are, so the gurus and consultants would have us believe, patterns and approaches that work, that have transformed well known companies and that now can do the same for your organisation. You are not alone: the challenges you face are ones others have faced before, so it makes sense to distil their experience and draw the necessary lessons.

This is how change management thinking has developed in the last 30 years. The approach has considerable strengths. It has focused management attention on the issues of change. For many organisations 'more of the same' has ceased to be an option. Order of magnitude improvements in performance have been needed and have demanded radical upheavals in structures, systems, working processes, skills and strategy. Change programmes have helped management understand the scale of the task and the interlocking nature of the different factors in play. They have encouraged managers to stand back from the familiar operational and strategic issues and think about management in a new light: how to bring about long-term shifts in the nature of their organisations.

They have helped management see the degree of will and determination often needed in processes of change. Those who want to shape the future must be prepared to keep pressing on when others are discouraged or ambivalent.

Change programmes have helped managers see the importance of focus and clarity, pushing them to think through what they want to change and how. Many management teams have been encouraged to develop a shared understanding of what they are trying to achieve. The attention paid to communication has pushed managers into talking to people throughout the organisation about goals and direction and, sometimes, to do more listening. The emphasis on planning and programming has encouraged managers to anticipate problems, to prepare what can be prepared and to consider the best sequence for change activities. The reference to best practice elsewhere has challenged the belief that 'our organisation is different' and pushed managers to look outside their own organisation and industry to see what can be learnt from very different organisations.

THE PROBLEMS WITH CHANGE PROGRAMMES

Yet in real life there are nagging problems, problems we see in one organisation after another. Most change efforts we have observed are neither complete successes nor abject failures. They are somewhere in the middle of the range: some clear gains, some disappointments but with a strong tinge of frustration, a sense that despite enormous investments of time, energy and money the efforts have not paid off as hoped. We meet many managers who are exhausted and frustrated, bruised and battered by the endless new projects and initiatives designed to 'bring about' change, yet who are never quite happy with the results. They often say that 'managing change' is the essence of their jobs: yet the business of how to 'manage change' remains mysterious in many ways. Let's look at what these problems are.

Unintended consequences

The first problem is how often unintended consequences accompany and sometimes displace the intended consequences of change. We worked with the chief executive of one international manufacturing group who was determined to restore the fortunes of his group, once the technological leader in its field but now finding its profitability under pressure as competitors eroded its quality and product edge. To encourage divisions to improve their performance, each year he selected an area on which he required them to focus and improve. One year it was manufacturing, another it was distribution, another it was human resource management. Demanding objectives were agreed for each division in the required area of focus. The chief executive's logic about the need for focus and rapid improvement in the chosen areas was impeccable, as were his awareness and understanding of best thinking and practice in each area.

Yet the unintended consequence of the approach was that increasingly divisional executives found it difficult to have an honest discussion with the group chief executive about their priorities or progress. They felt obliged to produce plans for the year's area of focus, even if they actually felt other issues were more important to the success of their division. Once an area had been 'done', they found it hard to admit to their continuing shortcomings in that area. One division, for example, had problems with its manufacturing processes but felt unable to discuss its plans because the key steps to achieve 'world-class manufacturing' were supposed to have been put in place several years ago. Increasingly, reviews with the chief executive became ordeals and it was difficult to share hopes and concerns for the business openly.

Another example is Britain's Health Service. The British government has instituted a series of 'reforms' aimed, among other things, at reducing bureaucracy and passing more responsibility to local managers, who are more responsive, it is hoped, to local conditions and the needs of patients. Independent trusts have been set up, an internal market established and local general practitioner doctors given more scope to run their own affairs. Yet, when undertaking a study on health promotion, we were struck by how widespread the perception is among local managers and doctors that senior managers treat them like children. Managers and doctors feel overwhelmed by a succession of central initiatives, not trusted, and monitored and controlled more than ever before. As one local manager put it to us: 'I spend most of my day ticking the boxes – doing what headquarters wants me to do. It's only when I've finished with that that I can get on with my real work, which is helping local health teams.'

The gap in perception between leaders and followers

In change efforts we have often met a gap in perception between those who initiate change and those who respond. The word 'change' itself is interpreted in very different ways. Senior managers often talk about the imperatives of change in the sense of responding to changed customers, markets and stakeholders. For the people they manage, 'change' can seem like another piece of management speak, a mantra that is muttered from time to time to justify confusing and exhausting reorganisations and new initiatives. In one company we met a manager who told us that she wasn't interested 'in all this stuff about change. We covered it in a workshop I attended last year.'

A headmistress at a London school told staff soon after appointment that her job was to 'manage change' in the organisation. She announced that a fundamental and radical overhaul of the school was necessary. The environment of the school was not properly cared for, she said, there wasn't enough discipline, nor enough 'love', and the administration needed much tightening up. She set in train a series of new initiatives and changes, for example weekly supervisions for teachers and regular inspections of the school grounds. Within a few months there was bitter hostility from the teachers. What they heard was not a determined effort to improve but a denigration of everything they had done in the past and an unwillingness to confront the realities of running an inner city school. The proposals the head was making did not connect with the reality as perceived by these teachers. Instead of considering what improvements they wanted to make, the teachers became absorbed in resisting the head.

Another example is the field of pay and rewards. Managers often offer incentives for particular behaviour only to be surprised when the new scheme is counterproductive. In one company, the managing director instituted 'Challenge 92', a competition between departments for the highest output rates and lowest errors. A few months later it had to be withdrawn after howls of protest from staff, who pointed out that the competition acted as a disincentive to the essential cooperation between functions. They also showed how managers had fudged figures in order to please their bosses. As the saying goes: 'What gets measured gets manipulated.'

Change is 'messy'

Transformation efforts have an uncomfortable habit of not working out as intended. Shifts in the way people think and work do not happen in a neat, orderly, programmed fashion. The 'Five Stages of Corporate Renewal' or the 'Fourteen Steps to Nirvana', so often advocated by consultants and academics, break down in practice. While their frameworks may illustrate certain points, they make change too neat. They understate the sheer contrariness of people and organisations.

The reality of organisational change is not tidy. As experienced managers know, the path is confused and uncertain, strewn with obstacles and unexpected difficulties. It is not something that can be planned and predicted. It is a process which evolves. Successful managers start with a strong sense of the direction in which they want to move but unsure of how to get there or how fast they can go. They are constantly adjusting their course to hold on to their chosen direction. Indeed, sometimes as they proceed they change their view of where they want to get to.

One reason they have to keep adjusting course is that the world moves on: just when a company has improved its performance it finds its competitors have as well and the hoped-for competitive advantage has crumbled to dust.

Vision – one step from hallucination

The unintended consequences of change programmes are much in evidence when companies seek to vision their way to the future. We are struck by how often visions simply don't work: they don't inspire, they don't encourage, they are viewed with cynicism by many or most within an organisation. They often become part of 'management speak', phrases and words which the ambitious become adept at using but which have lost any meaning they may once have had for the majority.

We can think of one insurance company where the management team locked itself away for a day to consider the objectives of the recently appointed chief executive and to formulate a new vision for the organisation. The session was compelling: people seemed to talk frankly about past disappointments and frustrations and spoke in a personal way about their aspirations for the company. After some initial hesitation, but driven on by the chief executive, a vision statement was formulated. It wasn't easy: participants found it difficult not to use management 'buzzwords' like excellence and quality, which it was agreed were too vague and didn't express specifically enough what the team wanted to achieve. Nevertheless, by the end a statement had been drafted. It wasn't perfect, people said, and would need reworking, but it was a creditable first draft and seemed to command a good deal of support from around the table.

What happened next – or rather what didn't – was what was most interesting. Instead of being seen as a rallying point for all those in the organisation who wanted change, the impact of the vision statement as it was shared around the organisation was either blank or negative. For some the vision was just another management exercise, something you had to live with but with no effect on the way work was done in practice.

Others reacted with hostility. How dare a new chief executive come in from another company and start talking about quality and customer service? What did he think managers and staff had been doing in the past? Did he have no understanding of their efforts to maintain quality in the face of intense pressure? And what was now stopping them from providing quality, except the new output targets and staff reductions imposed by this same chief executive?

It emerged that what was valuable about preparing the vision statement was the process the management team had been through. They had learnt about each other and, while formulating the vision, come closer together and understood more of their common aspirations. Those who had not participated in developing the vision were left cold by it: to them the words sounded like worthy, generalised aspirations, not a guide to conduct and action in the here and now. It was not something they had helped shape so they felt no 'ownership' of it.

We have seen these same problems in many organisations. First there is the difficulty of developing distinctive visions with some bite to them. So many vision statements sound generalised, exhortative, too ill defined and undeniable to be effective. If you say you are in favour of quality and customer service, so what? Who isn't? So many management words have become devalued, robbed of all meaning.

Isn't it curious that so many visions are the same? How do so many organisations, despite all their differences of history, environment and culture, come to the same words about quality, customer service, valuing people and the rest of it? What chance does a company have of competing successfully if its objectives mirror those of its competitors?

In some cases the visions, however banal, are printed on plastic cards, included in videos, stuck on the wall in reception areas, put up around factories and offices and included in the annual report. Employees can come to feel a sense of embarrassment about the vision statement and pretend it doesn't exist – a bit like the member of the family with anti-social habits whom you hope no one will notice!

Often the vision seems overwhelming to people within the organisation. Instead of being energised, people are left feeling depressed: knowing the difficulties and frustrations of day-to-day operations, they sense that the vision, with its idealised picture of the future, is unattainable. 'How can we ever turn the organisation we know into the paragon described in the vision?' they ask.

What frequently happens is that the vision is developed and communicated (at least to some extent) but then not followed up. It is supposed to guide strategy and operations but somehow is lost sight of under the pressure of day-to-day priorities. Employees nod intelligently but gain no clear picture of what change is intended. The key step of testing the aspirations against reality is often ignored: 'What does this vision mean to you? What difference will it make? How will you act differently?'

Very often employees contrast the beliefs espoused in the vision with the management behaviour and decisions they experience. Vision then becomes a stick with which to beat management. The gap that is sure to exist between the intention set out in the vision and and the current behaviour and decisions of managers is bound to be noticed and thrown in managers' faces. Employees ask: 'How can you expect us to take this vision seriously when you, the managers, are not living up to it?'

Repeated rescues

One of the strongest images of managing change is of heroic chief executives riding to the rescue of ailing companies. They arrive from outside, determined to bring to an end a period of decline and to renew the organisation. They carry the answer to the company's problems in their knapsack: even before appointment they were able to identify the key problems and with a little first-hand experience they are able in the first 100 days to see what has to be done. Thereafter it is mainly a question of effective implementation: communicating incessantly their vision of renewal and pushing through the changes needed. They act swiftly, often moving people, bringing in their own team, making key symbolic changes in the critical first period in the post and acting with a decisiveness and energy that were lacking in the old regime. If they are true heroes, their formula is right and after months or even years of struggle they win through, transforming companies and gaining the reputations to go on to even larger responsibilities in the future.

It's a beguiling picture. But how often is it true? Even when chief executives succeed in turning around companies, is it more than a caricature of what has happened? How is it that only a few years after a triumphant turnaround some companies are back in deep trouble?

Chrysler is a company that has come back from the (nearly) dead. In 1990, for the second time in only five years, it faced bankruptcy: in the last quarter of 1989 it had made a loss of $664 million, its product range was so antiquated that its products could only be sold at heavy discounts, frequently at a loss, and it was embarking on plans to close a third of its capacity and sack a third of its workers. By 1994 the company had returned to healthy profitability and its new small car, the Neon, was attracting such respectful attention from Toyota that the Japanese company summoned a special meeting of engineers and suppliers to study how the car had been made.

How had it been done? Not by the charismatic Lee Iacocca, who had given way in January 1993 to Robert Eaton, a very different leader. In his first address to managers after taking over as chief executive, Mr Eaton 'entertained his audience with eight quotations about Chrysler's dramatic recovery. Each sounded as though it had been written recently. In fact, as he revealed, the first was from 1952, the last from 1983. Chrysler had been through eight crises in between. "We have got to quit getting sick," said Mr Eaton. "I want to be the first chairman in the history of Chrysler not to have to lead the company back from the brink of bankruptcy."' As *The Economist* put it:

Chrysler's turnaround resulted not from a grand corporate strategy handed down from on high, but from top management's decision to employ the wisdom already embedded in the organisation...it was a story of how middle managers deep in the organisation glimpsed the way forward, and how their superiors eventually understood what they were doing and gave them the tools they needed.

Mistaking structure for organisation

Another real-life problem with change programmes is managers acting as if structural change – changing roles and responsibilities on the organisation chart – is the key to transformation. It's an old fallacy in a new guise. Over 15 years ago McKinsey's developed the '7-S' model to demonstrate that organisation is about much more than structure: it is also shaped by strategy, systems (how things are done, much more than just computer systems), staff, skills, shared values and management style. More recently Bob Waterman has shown how successful companies have 'baked in' ways of liberating more of the talent of their people and delivering greater value to customers: the key to which are patterns of behaviour and thinking that reach far beyond organisational structure. In many places it is the unwritten rules which shape what people do much more than the formal job titles or role descriptions.

Yet still the pattern persists of managers changing structures and expecting transformation to follow. When one reorganisation does not deliver the expected benefits, it's on to the next one. In the 1970s it was divisionalisation, for a while strategic business units ruled supreme, now there is process-based organisation – no more functional directors, no more turf battles, no more interdepartmental fighting, just smooth, effective cross-business processes. The passion for cross-functional organisation is no more than the latest stage in this evolution. Already managers are finding that this type of organisation is easy to draw but much more difficult to create in reality.

Frequently reorganisations get in the way of change rather then enabling it. While reorganisation is pending, managers turn inwards, looking to see how they can protect their current position or carve out a larger one. They focus on the internal politics of the organisation, on whom to please and how. They often lose sight of the external objectives that are meant to be the purpose of the change. We meet many managers sagging under the pressure of constant reorganisations, unsure what their current role is, exhausted by the internal battles, fearful for their futures. We meet others who are immobilised by fear, traumatised by one reorganisation after another and incapable for the moment of doing anything but react to events.

The impact of some reorganisations is summed up by a story of the man who arrived home late one night to be greeted by his young son. 'Why are you late, Daddy?' asked the boy. 'I've been working on the latest reorganisation,' his father said. 'What's a reorganisation, Daddy?' 'I'll show you,' said the father and took his son out into the back garden where there was a large tree. Suddenly the father clapped his hands loudly. All the birds which had been sitting in the tree flew away. A few moments later they began to come back and after a while the tree was full again of birds but in different positions. '*That*, my son, is a reorganisation.'

Navel gazing

A tendency to become internally absorbed is another paradox of efforts aimed at improving the external effectiveness of the organisation.

When David Palk became General Manager of ICL Product Distribution in 1988, the company was in the middle of a company-wide quality initiative. Yet at the same time service levels to customers were abysmal. Only 27 per cent of complete orders were delivered to customers on time. 'What I found was people sitting in quality meetings discussing the price of coffee at vending machines, while customer orders continued to run late,' says David. 'The first thing I did was to get people out of those meetings and attending instead to the needs of customers. In those early days we had one objective only: to deliver 100 per cent on time.'

IBM was one of the original practitioners of total quality management, which is aimed at least in theory at achieving high levels of customer satisfaction. Yet even that company decided in 1989 – three years before its crash into losses – that its quality efforts had been focused too much internally. The quality initiative was relaunched as 'Market Driven Quality'.

Strangely the more inward the focus, often the more frenetic the activity. In order to measure and control the change efforts, senior managers ask for reports of how many groups have met, how many suggestions made, how many newsletters issued. The change initiative becomes an industry in its own right, and the focus slips from business results to change activities. As a Roman general is reported to have said: 'Having lost sight of our goals, we redoubled our efforts.'

Programmitis

Which book is my boss going to read on holiday this year? That's what I worry about. What new fad or theory is he going to pick up and try to impose on us when he gets back?
                              Manager in a large services company

The pattern of frenetic change activity – and disappointing results – has reached its zenith with the current passion for change programmes, particularly in large organisations. There is a continuing interest in magic solutions to organisational problems. Just when you thought total quality management was dying away, along comes business process reengineering. Whatever the cynicism about the formulas, the conferences continue to be full, the books keep selling. The idea that someone somewhere already has the answer to your problem, that you take it and plug it into your organisation like a domestic appliance, continues to be attractive.

To take the latest craze of reengineering, the level of activity is staggering. A study of 624 companies by CSC Index found that 75 per cent of European companies had at least one reengineering project on the go and that half of those who didn't were planning to have one in the near future. It is quite difficult to find a manager over 30 years old in a large company who hasn't been 'done' by a change programme of some sort and who hasn't acquired a certain cynicism as a result. Often people learn the words, play the game and carry on as before.

The phenomenon of programmes does not stop with just one effort. As one programme reaches its plateau – and often before it has – managers launch other programmes. In recent years large organisations in both the private and public sectors have been through a succession of change initiatives. In the most extreme cases this becomes the scourge of 'programmitis', an ever-increasing number of programmes and initiatives. One company we worked with had 19 initiatives going at once. In their anxiety to push through change, senior managers try harder with more exhortation and more demands for staff to shift their thinking and behaviour. They search around for new mechanisms to push through what they want and new banners to work under. The less the programmes work, the more senior managers pile on new initiatives.

THE CONSEQUENCES

Frustration and exhaustion

The result of this plethora of change programmes is corporate – and individual – exhaustion. People in an organisation become bewildered by the range of change initiatives, unsure about the priorities they are supposed to work to. The different change initiatives often seem inconsistent. There is a sense of imposition – 'we're doing this because we've been told to' – and a corresponding reduction in the energy and commitment that go into achieving the desired changes.

In the most serious cases, the pattern of increasing 'change' activities and mounting frustration is fuelled by managers' sense of insecurity. As one MD admitted, 'the more self doubt we have, the more arrogant we become. The less confident we are of our ability to solve the problems, the less we are prepared to involve others and listen to them.'

The pattern of insecurity and relentless activity is sometimes mirrored at different levels of an organisation. Managers who are the victims of change initiatives imposed from above become persecutors of staff below them. In Britain's NHS we have found feelings and actions at one level which reflect exactly those of managers below and above. Just as regional managers feel insecure and complain that their HQ does not listen and keeps imposing unrealistic changes, so district managers complain about the regional ones, doctors complain about district managers and nurses about doctors.

And the less the change programmes work, the more managers try to control developments. They ask for more and more measurement and reporting – often of the change activities, not of the substance of change they are seeking. This leads to a contradiction. Change initiatives come to rely heavily on control, which defeats their supposed objectives of empowering people and encouraging learning.

Ironically, change programmes often place an impossible burden on senior managers. They have to supply the energy for change. They have to find the formula for success. They have to be latter-day Churchills inspiring people to transform their behaviour. And the less it works the harder they try. No wonder some managers describe managing change as pushing water uphill! And it's no surprise they are exhausted.

Ultimately change programmes implies an *instrumental* view of change. They are based on the belief that change is *done to* organisations, that people at the top can know the answer and then apply it to the organisation. But what if fundamental change – the transformation that occurs when people change their mental maps of the world – cannot be predicted? What if it is inherently uncertain and the mental models of those seeking to lead change are as much subject to change as those who follow? What if transformation *cannot* be managed – what can be put in the place of change programmes?

In Chapter 3 we explore two very different ways of thinking about fundamental change, and suggest how we can move beyond these to 'lean into the future'.

3

Flawed Assumptions about Change

It would be tempting to say that the problems we describe in Chapter 2 are the result of faulty implementation: that it is not change programmes which are wrong but the way they are handled. We think not. The problems are too common, they form too much of a pattern for that to be a satisfactory answer. Instead it is the thinking on which change programmes are based which needs to be reexamined, not in fact because it is wrong, but because it does not take account of the whole picture of people and organisations. It is a partial view, one that works for a time but ultimately leads to frustration.

COMPARING TWO DIFFERENT MODELS OF CHANGE

In this chapter we look in turn at the critical assumptions which under-pin two very different ways of considering change. First we look at the assumptions made if organisations are seen as machines, as happens with the change programmes described in Chapter 2. Then we look at the assumptions made if organisations are viewed as living systems: self-organising, dynamic and with a natural capacity to make the most of the environments they are in. In this second view, individuals cannot 'manage' change. Trying to achieve shifts in thinking and behaviour is too subtle, too unpredictable a process for it to be possible to manage it. The best individuals can do is 'work with' change, responding to it and seeking to influence it.

Finally we suggest how to move beyond the black and white choices involved in these two sets of assumptions to explore another way of working with change. This is what we call 'leaning into the future' – a combination of leading *and* learning.

ORGANISATIONS AS MACHINES

'Change needs to be driven'

The first assumption we very often hear when organisations are seen as machines is that change in the patterns of an organisation needs to be made to happen. Without some push, some injection of energy, nothing will shift. The words that are used are telling: managers talk of 'forcing', 'driving through', 'bringing about' change. Many of the metaphors are ones of violence and force. There is a clear assumption that the energy needs to come from outside the mass of the organisation, usually from top management, sometimes from outsiders such as shareholders or the government.

> *We've worked hard now on quality for several years. We've had our successes: people are much more aware. They understand what quality is now. And yet somehow the initiative has plateaued. The excitement and energy has gone out of it. Do you have any ideas on how we could remarket the initiative, get it moving again, show people how important it still is? Can you help?*

This comment came to us from the quality director of a household-name company. It's a request we receive quite often: how can we reenergise a flagging change effort?

The assumption is that change has to be made to happen. There is, it is said, a natural inertia in people and organisations. People are inherently conservative, it is asserted. They prefer what they are familiar with: they also have vested interests and positions to defend. They are naturally fearful that any change will leave them worse off than before. In addition, there are some people in every organisation who will block change or try to sabotage it. These are the 'resistors' of change: they must be managed, minimised and, if necessary, removed from their jobs if the change process is to be successful.

It is also often said that we live in an era of unprecedented change. The pace of technological developments, the speed of communications, the removal of barriers to the global economy mean that managers must act fast to change their companies before they are overwhelmed by events. A series of best-selling business books have started from this premise. *In Search of Excellence* by Peters and Waterman, *The Change Masters* by Moss Kanter and *Reengineering the Corporation* by Hammer and Champy all follow this pattern. Tom Peters coined the term 'The Nanosecond Nineties' to indicate that the one requirement of organisations now is that they should be fleet of foot, and much of the literature about the 'learning organisation' argues that learning needs to become the key capability of organisations because markets and environments are now changing so fast.

Against this background there is always more for managers to do: more initiatives to launch, more to communicate, more difficult decisions to take. Managers can never relax. One of the most popular images we hear is that of change as a journey, with no fixed departure point and no definite arrival. When you have climbed one mountain, there looming in front of you is the next summit. Always, it seems, there is a new mountain to conquer.

'Change starts with visioning'

We discussed in Chapter 2 the central role that visioning plays in change programmes. It is assumed that the challenge is for leaders to develop and communicate clear and coherent visions of the future which can then provide a beacon for the efforts of others. Effective visions are said to inspire: they enable staff to see where the organisation is going and how their efforts fit with those of others. They provide 'the context for designing and managing the change goals and the effort needed to bridge the gap to meet those goals.' In particular, vision provides the template against which plans and programmes can be measured. Do proposals 'align' with the vision? Without visioning, it is said, organisations will not change in the ways needed, will not adapt and prosper in changing environments.

'The answer is out there'

If managers feel under pressure to drive change through and to create effective visions, help is at hand in the further assumption that the answer, the way in which your organisation needs to change and how, is already available. There are a limited number of situations and challenges you can face. If you look long enough and hard enough, some 'excellent company', some guru or consultant, can tell you how to handle it. We mentioned in Chapter 2 how extraordinarily popular business process reengineering has become. If you don't like reengineering, there are programmes to reduce cost, improve quality, develop continuous improvement, 'delayer' and 'downsize', improve customer service, empower employees, change culture, develop vision and values, 'delight' customers. And while cynicism about the 'magic bullet' answers grows, still the business books sell as never before, the consultancies continue to expand, the conferences continue to be well attended. Coming next: the impact of complexity theory?

The view is that the answer must exist because it is just a matter of logic and of special expertise in 'change management'. Thus those who helped transform customer service at British Airways or quality at Xerox are eagerly sought out by other organisations. Also coming soon: an active market in managers who can claim success in reengineering?

'You have to start afresh'

The essence of this assumption is that each of the answers is new, radical, transcends all that went before it. The logic is clear: if people are to change the way they view their work and organisation, a clean break with the past is needed. As Joel Barker, who has popularised the notion of 'paradigms', the mental frameworks we use to make sense of the world, says: 'When the paradigm shifts, we all go down to zero. Past expertise does not carry over.'

Reengineering – sweeping away the past

The belief that the past needs to be uprooted has reached a peak with the current craze for reengineering. In its rhetoric at least – much less in its practice – reengineering demands that companies reinvent themselves. Reengineering, say Hammer and Champy, is 'starting over. It is about beginning again with a clean sheet of paper. It is about rejecting conventional wisdom and received assumptions of the past... it is about reversing the industrial revolution... tradition counts for nothing. Reengineering is a new beginning.' Its key words are 'fundamental', 'radical', 'dramatic' and 'process'.

The last person to use language like this was China's Chairman Mao in the Cultural Revolution. He too insisted on sweeping away the past. Priceless artifacts, codes of conduct, norms of human behaviour developed over centuries: all had to be smashed before he could create his perfect society. 'Destroy to build' was his motto. The ways of the past were utterly wrong. There had to be an uprooting, a tearing away from the past before the future could be created.

This was, after all, the logic of communism taken to its extreme: the idea that the future could be rationally planned and that the past was of no account. It's ironic that when communism has almost died, its thought process should reappear inside Western companies. What is reengineering but the 'planned economy' reappearing on a smaller scale?

Our view is that successful organisations do not deny or seek to destroy the inheritance of the past. Instead, they seek to build on it. They attempt to understand in depth why they have been successful and they try to do more of it. They are respectful of the learning accumulated from experience, much of which they recognise is not made explicit at the top of the organisation. They acknowledge their faults but try to see them in balance with their good qualities. Their desire to change is based on self-confidence and self-belief, not denigration of what they have been.

'Everyone is for change – for others'

The terms of the requests for help we receive are often the same: how to sell, market, put new energy into the change managers want to do *to* the organisation. Senior managers see a need for *other people* to care more about customers, work harder, control costs better, change their ways of working. The assumption is that top managers have the answer. They're OK. The challenge is to get the others – sometimes other senior managers, often middle managers and shopfloor workers – to adopt the change.

In the 1980s many banks and insurance companies set up customer service programmes with the idea that they could train their staff to perform better. The analysis went: our customer service is inadequate – we need to improve it. The service is poor because the staff do not care or do not understand the importance of providing excellent service – the solution is to put all staff through a customer service programme, then they will understand and know what to do, and service will improve.

Often the assumptions of those further down the hierarchy mirror those of senior managers. They too see change as an issue for others; they also see others as the blockage. In the case of middle managers it can be front-line staff and senior managers themselves; in the case of front-line workers, all managers, particularly first-level supervisors.

'Change can be planned and predicted'

The multi-step approaches, the gap analysis, the 'change management' steering groups, the emphasis on aligning activities with the vision, the careful monitoring and control which we described in Chapter 2 are all indicative of the assumption that change can be planned and predicted. If the answer – the pattern of priorities and actions that will enable an organisation to succeed – is known, then the rest is merely a matter of implementation. It needs to be planned carefully, the requisite responsibilities and resources have to be assigned, progress must be monitored: essentially 'change management' becomes a huge project. The scale of the task and of the issues involved may seem intimidating, but senior executives can look to the well-understood disciplines of project management to help them achieve the desired results.

Organisations as machines

Taken together, the assumptions we have examined – that change is done *to* organisations by those with vision, that it needs to be driven, that the answer is 'out there', that the past needs to be swept away, that others need to change and that transformation processes can be planned and predicted – are characteristic of a mechanical view of organisations. This is a metaphor which keeps reappearing. More than 30 years after Burns and Stalker identified the limitations of the machine metaphor for organisations, that analogy proves astonishingly persistent. It still underlies much current practice of 'change management'. The signals are the words people use: managers and consultants talk about 'pushing' or 'driving through' change, they describe 'barriers' and 'obstacles' and identify the 'resistance' to change and how they must be 'overcome'. They identify 'levers for change' and talk about the need to 'generate momentum'. They draw pictures of motor cars and flywheels.

The idea is of a machine which can be designed and built, driven and controlled. And now, of course, 'reengineered'.

Yet the mechanical analogy is inadequate. Organisations are living things with personalities and histories. They contain people with all their richness and complexity. They are subtle systems. Cause and effect are not linear. If you make a change in one place, unintended consequences may arise at some remove, both in distance and in time. If you focus on one element in isolation, you are likely to be frustrated. The only way to try and understand is to look at the whole. Fortunately, that is what the intuition in all of us does naturally – provided we are prepared to use it.

ORGANISATIONS AS LIVING SYSTEMS

An alternative view is to see organisations as living systems. Instead of the mechanical metaphor, what would it mean if organisations were regarded as organisms which live and die, grow and decline and whose species evolve? What if the latest thinking in biology and ecology were considered? What implications would this have?

It would suggest that organizations were *adaptive*. Living systems are not passive; they try to turn events to their advantage. Thus species in the natural world have an innate capacity to evolve to make the most of the changing environment. This view suggests that patterns of behaviour and thinking shift of their own accord, sometimes slowly, sometimes quickly, under the pressure of events.

Adopting this view would encourage us to look at the *self-organising* properties of organisations: elements within a system adapt to each other and acquire collective properties without anyone willing it to happen. Thus the millions of cells in a person's skin maintain an equilibrium, develop and age without anyone being in charge or consciously organising it.

It would suggest that organisations were *interdependent* with their environment, interacting with it in complex ways, being influenced by it and shaping it.

And it would draw attention to the *dynamic* nature of organisations. They are obviously alive. They are constantly balancing the need for order and coherence (which taken too far leads to rigidity) and for flexibility (which taken too far leads to anarchy).

Given this alternative model, let's look at what it would imply for managers seeking to transform their organisations.

'Change is natural, but not easy!'

In living systems change occurs as a natural phenomenon all the time. The environment changes, individuals age, change in patterns of behaviour and thinking is happening all the time without anyone necessarily willing it to occur. Gareth Morgan in his book *Images of Organization* quotes from the Greek philosopher Heraclitus, who argued around 500 BC that the universe is in a constant state of flux, embodying characteristics of permanence and change. He said:

You cannot step twice into the same river, for other waters are continually flowing on... Everything flows and nothing abides; everything gives way and nothing stays fixed... Cool things become warm, the warm grows cool; the moist dries, the parched becomes moist... It is in changing that things find repose.

In the case of changes in the norms of thinking and behaviour in organisations, the change may sometimes seem very slow, particularly to those involved, conscious of the patterns day to day. To an outsider, able to step back and look at shifts over months and years, the change in attitudes and behaviour can seem very rapid.

The living systems view would acknowledge that adjusting to change is often painful. Change may be happening all the time but adapting to it is still difficult. It is not easy to give up familiar ways of thinking and acting. People who have had to let go of failed relationships, those who have had to find new ways of working when made redundant, people who have given up the expectations of parents and learnt to work to their own goals, know how hard this letting go can be.

The same applies to organisations. One of the problems with many large organisations is that they take on new priorities and initiatives but do not let go of the old. They do not make space, both physical and psychological, for the new initiatives. One company we worked in had built success on product quality markedly superior to that of its competitors. Over the years its product edge had eroded as competitors caught up. Yet managers found it very hard to see their product as a commodity and shift to other priorities of cost reduction or service improvement. For them there had to be some way of recapturing the golden age when customers had flocked to buy their product, despite higher prices and poor service.

The living systems thinking suggests there is a potential appetite for change in all organisations. What if workers wanted to improve and have been prevented by blocks which the organisation has put in their way? How many of us are happy to do a poor job, to know that customers are dissatisfied, that we are not giving of our best?

My experience is that Kaizen [continuous improvement] comes naturally to people on the shop floor. When you encourage workers to improve quality they always ask: 'why didn't you do it before? For years we've pointed out the mistakes that are being made but no one listened to us.'

Peter Willats, founder of the Kaizen Institute of Europe

The pride is naturally there; the job of managers is to release it. Often our systems of measurement and our short term horizons get in the way. We have to...clear them out of the way.

Barry Morgans of IBM

As consultants we frequently enable people who would otherwise have been ignored to participate in projects and often find that once drawn in they are enthusiastic advocates of change. Several years ago we worked in a manufacturing business on a cost-reduction exercise. One of the accountants in the company was a 50-year-old man, cynical and resentful, passed over a number of times for promotion because of his lack of formal qualifications and the perception that he was an awkward so-and-so. Yet he had worked in the company for 20 years: he knew the business backwards and the life story of most people who worked in it. We suggested that he be seconded to the project. Within a few weeks he had become its most valuable member. He was incisive, practical and persuasive and he worked hard to help the team. His whole approach switched round. For the first time in many years, simply by being included in the team and being listened to as a member of it, he felt valued.

Thus the living systems view is that the challenge is not to *drive* change but to *release* the potential for change, leading and encouraging it in the directions that will help the organisation to flourish. It suggests that there are few organisations that do not already have energy to change. Some of it is in people's hopes and aspirations, some in their frustrations and concerns, but it is there. The issue for leaders becomes one of removing the constraints to innovation and adaptation and of channelling and connecting the desire for change. Understanding exactly what the constraints are and why they have arisen is the key to 'unsticking' the organisation and releasing latent energy for change.

'Don't be anxious about change'

The living systems view challenges the widely held belief that we live in an era of unprecedented change. Change is inherent in the growth and decline, evolution and death of living systems. The anxiety about unprecedented rates of change helps no one except the consultants and gurus. It suggests that the enormous pressure to change being placed on organisations by books, conferences and consultants is artificial and the activity they generate does not help organisations. Henry Mintzberg in his book *The Rise and Fall of Strategic Planning* asks: 'Why does every generation have to think that it lives in the period with the greatest turbulence?'

The living systems thinking suggests that much of the 'change' which organisations are undergoing is self-inflicted: the result of managers desperate to force change through instead of working with the natural capacity of people and organisations to develop. It suggests that by working against the grain of organisations managers waste time and energy. If they could find ways to tap the natural potential of people to develop, they would save themselves a lot of frustration and avoid unnecessary pain and anger among the recipients of the 'change initiatives'.

The distinction between change in behaviour and thinking and 'change' as part of management speak is well illustrated by an example from Britain's National Health Service. We recently studied the impact of the government's efforts to make doctors undertake more health promotion. One of the most striking findings was the separation – in the minds of doctors, nurses and managers – between what was being done to keep those in authority happy and what was felt to be 'real health promotion'. One doctor described: 'All the contracts and collection of statistics hasn't made any difference to what I actually do. I continue – as I have always done – to try and change, opportunistically, my patients' behaviour when I think it can do some good. Anything more than that is just unrealistic.'

The living systems view says that the pressure for incessant change also overlooks the need for stability. No organisation and no individual can cope with complete uncertainty, having all their key beliefs and norms forever open to question. We need periods of relative stability and we need areas of certainty. We need to be clear about what we know as well as what we don't know. And that's the natural pattern of transformation. Periods of rapid change are interspersed with long periods of relative stability. To suggest, as some management writers like Tom Peters appear to, that everything needs to be up for grabs, all the time, is a recipe for madness.

'Awareness of current reality'

The living systems view shifts attention from looking at aspirations for the future to becoming clearer about current reality. A problem with visions is indeed that they often seem disconnected from the reality staff see around them. Employees feel that the vision denigrates the present and the past of the organisation. By talking about the idealised future the vision seems to ignore the pressures and difficulties people have faced. Staff who have made their career with the organisation derive part of their sense of self-worth from its achievements and their identity with it. They now feel undermined and angry: their work appears not to be valued. They often also feel both depressed and guilty because they cannot live up to the lofty aspirations set out in the vision. And the only people who really take responsibility for the vision and its implementation are those few who developed it.

Most disturbingly, the living systems perspective challenges the idea that change is a process of activity aimed at a particular outcome. Instead, it suggests that organisations are too subtle, the interdependencies within an organisation and between the organisation and its environment are too involved for managers to be able to shape the future in this way. 'Shaping the future' is a fantasy of control. Managers need to let go of the idea that they can control the future: instead they should be as true as they can to their own convictions and seek to live in harmony with the world around them.

Advocates of this view even deny that intention exists apart from action. They see managers as expressing their true intention in the actions they take; if their intention shifts their actions also will. What is important, therefore, is not any statement of vision but the pattern of actions and behaviour: these reveal what managers really believe.

Instead of developing unreal wish lists in the form of visions, managers should consider the capacity of their organisation to respond to change. They should work to remove the obstacles or constraints that reduce an organisation's capacity to respond. Species and organisations do not develop independently: they evolve together, turning to advantage the opportunities created by others' development. The health of an organisation is closely related to the health of its environment: in attending to its environment, an organisation is attending to itself. If leaders are keenly aware of changes in the environment and in other companies or organisations, they can anticipate the opportunities that may arise. It is important to ask: 'How can we gain advantage from the developments of others? What could we do that might be mutually beneficial?'

'The answer is within'

As living systems, organisations have their own personalities and histories. Every organisation is different and has particular reasons for developing as it has. There is no one right way forward – it depends on the context of each system and environment. What one company or organisation may find a good solution in one context may not work for another.

There are no excellent companies. Organisations need to let go of the idea that there are paragons out there which they can copy. Just like individuals, organisations need to find their own reasons to change. Being told to change – by a guru, consultant or chief executive – is a fruitless exercise. Trying to emulate another organisation is as foolish as an individual seeking to copy another person's way of living.

'Reinforce emerging patterns'

Because each organisation is different, it is important to look carefully at the reasons for an organisation's past success and its current distinctive competences or capabilities. The patterns of thinking and behaviour in an organisation have developed for a reason. Systems have found a way to flourish in the environment they are in. Those that didn't no longer survive. There is a richness and subtlety in what has evolved, what has stood the test of time, which it may be difficult for any one actor to see. If you want to lead change, it is vital to understand in depth why the system has been successful. Starting by understanding the past and the present is the best way to prepare for the future.

So it is with other changes in behaviour and thinking. Often they are not willed to happen so much as *emerge*. The skill of leaders is not pathfinding in isolation but seeing the new pattern and directing attention to it. Rosabeth Moss Kanter in her book *The Change Masters* describes the vital role leaders play in rewriting the history of organisations. They make sense, she says, of what has gone before, picking out the themes and lessons that they want to emphasise now. History tells not so much about the past as about the present: what picture of the past current leaders wish to convey.

In *The Foundations of Corporate Success* John Kay argues that it is vital for a company to understand fully its 'distinctive capabilities', the things which it does well and which a competitor would find it difficult or impossible to copy. He castigates 'wish-driven' strategies: successful strategies, he says, come not from the realisation of visions and missions but from a careful appreciation of the strengths of the firm and the economic environment it faces. Creating distinctive capabilities is, by definition, very difficult; the more likely route to success is to appreciate fully what existing capabilities are and find a profitable outlet for them.

Leadership, therefore, is less concerned with *willing* organisations to change and more with working *with* change, listening, interpreting, making sense of what's happening and thereby encouraging and reinforcing trends which will help the organisation succeed.

'We need to change'

In a living system all the elements are changing together. The shift one element makes has a knock-on effect on others. The patterns of behaviour in one part of the system reflect the patterns in other parts and in the system as a whole.

Thus this view suggests that something else is needed for effective leadership of transformation: leaders strong enough to admit that they too are learning, that maybe they are part of – perhaps they *are* – the problem. We have often been asked by managements to help change their employees (so they care more about customers, are more cost conscious, take responsibility for improvement), only to find that a precondition of change in the organisation is that the management team itself changes.

Very often the attitudes that top managers complain about are merely the reflection of their own behaviour and thinking. One chief executive complained that his people never had any ideas and that all initiative had to come from him. What was his behaviour when people did occasionally put their heads above the parapet and offer a suggestion? He always had an answer: it couldn't be done for this reason or that; or he had already looked into it and it was impractical. The chief executive was right to think his style was open and accessible. What he did not appreciate was that people felt browbeaten by him. He was brighter than most of his managers and better informed. Why should anyone else take the initiative with such a boss?

The same is true for other people in organisations. Just as it is usually vital that senior managers see that they need to change, so also middle managers and front-line workers need to see that they have a part in change and that blaming problems on others leads nowhere.

If the living systems view is accurate, it would also suggest that management and business are not separate from the rest of the world, with their own norms and characteristics. The insights people learn in the rest of their lives are just as applicable to organisations. The wisdom we all accumulate through our adult lives, as we grow up, as we learn about ourselves and about others, as we bring up children, as we learn to cope with disasters and tragedies, opportunities and success, should be made available in the world of work. Instead of seeing our life in organisations as in a separate compartment, subject to different rules and assumptions and surrounded by the strange language of management and business, we should bring to bear our experience of life, apply the same rules and assumptions that work for us elsewhere.

'Live with uncertainty'

The evolution of living systems is inherently unpredictable; there are too many variables and too much interdependence to be sure about cause and effect. The future is shaped by actions and reactions, of which only a percentage can be predicted, a limited distance into the future. People must be prepared to work with the known *and* to respond to emerging opportunities.

In a process of radical organisational change the future is unknowable. The environment or markets in which the organisation will have to live in the future are unpredictable. It's an old saying that 'the only thing you can be sure about a forecast is that it is wrong'. The value of a forecast is not what it tells you about the future, but the light it sheds on where the organisation is now and the choices open to it.

The future is unknowable because the patterns of behaviour and thinking that will enable the organisation to thrive in that future environment have yet to be discovered.

In one healthcare company the agreed policy was that the company sold only treatments which were approved by the government for reimbursement to the patient. Otherwise patients paid the total cost of the treatment and this was thought to make the products unattractive. One day, visiting a local sales office, the Sales Director noticed that it had sold a drug not on the approved list. He found out that even though the drug was not approved it was an attractive product for doctor and patient alike. He asked other offices to promote the treatment and there too it sold well. The decision turned out to be the beginning of an important strategic change. The company came to develop what became, because of changes in government policy, a very important market. The change came not from analysis but from intelligent opportunism, spotting a successful change and encouraging others to follow it.

The new pattern was not something senior managers knew at the beginning of a process of change and passed on to the rest of the organisation. What happened was that the new pattern emerged from a welter of activities and tendencies. No one saw it clearly at the start. All – including top management – were learning together.

'Feelings and emotion are important'

Living systems thinking pushes us to see people as a whole: to consider their emotional and subconscious as well as their rational side.

Often people get stuck because their conscious need and wants are in conflict with unconscious forces and motivations. We are all aware that we are not always rational beings: at times our actions are driven by emotions and feelings and sometimes we don't know where these feelings come from.

The importance of this for change is, of course, that people do things for the strangest reasons. Rationality is often a poor guide. Some years ago we worked with a large packaging business on its strategy. At one session there was a fierce debate about whether to go after a big acquisition in the US. After animated discussion it was agreed that the logic was clear: the US had been a very attractive market, with weaker competition and higher prices, but this was changing fast. New entrants were coming into the market, the growth of consumer demand was slowing down and the outlook for profitability in the market was poor.

It was agreed that limited management resources should be focused on improving the company's competitive position in Europe.

What happened 10 days after the strategy review was completed? Two directors heard about a company in the US that was up for sale and promptly began a process that led eventually to its acquisition. What had happened to all those good reasons for not investing in the US? They were simply less powerful than the instinctive and personal judgements that the leading directors had made that the future of the company lay in the US.

Intuition is important. Often people know what to do but can't articulate why. They have an instinct, a feeling that they ought to do something or behave in a certain way. So also with change. In our experience managers have a great deal of instinct and intuition about what works and what doesn't. If they feel it is OK to discuss openly what their instinct tells them, there is a huge well of insights to be drawn from.

'Managers should try less hard'

The optimistic conclusion from applying the living systems thinking is that managers should try *less* hard when handling change. Most organisations, it is suggested, are full of energy for change. The problem is that most of it lacks a constructive outlet and therefore assumes negative forms: bitching, cynicism, defensiveness, territorial battles. Once some of it is converted to help the organisation rather than hinder it, the potential for change is great.

In one company we worked in the directors drove themselves unremittingly to improve the competitiveness of the business. They lived in a giddy whirl of activity, seeking to run the business and improve it at the same time. They rushed from project to project changing this system, that structure, and yet the patterns of thinking and behaviour remained the same. They were convinced that things only happened when they drove them forward themselves. They were perpetually frustrated by what they saw as the reactive and difficult behaviour of the mass of managers and staff.

Yet when we talked to middle managers and staff it was clear that there was intense energy for change at all levels. Staff were seething with anger at the way the company was run. They felt ignored, devalued, manipulated. Impressively, they had not given up on the company. They longed to succeed.

The issue was not how to supply the energy for change from above, but how to tap some of the energy already there. The message for senior managers was: 'Try less hard. Slow down. Listen to what's there.'

LEANING INTO THE FUTURE

We have drawn two sharply contrasting pictures of change and of what individuals can do. In the mechanical metaphor, managers push through transformation, applying known answers in a logical, sequenced way. In the living systems view, managers work with the forces that are already there and with patterns that emerge. They do not bring about change at all; they encourage responsiveness and learning.

Both pictures illuminate and have their limitations. They remain metaphors: they are not the whole truth, simply one way of understanding reality. A way of seeing is also a way of not seeing. The mechanical metaphor assumes that change is 'done to' organisations, that important shifts in thinking and behaviour can be planned and predicted, that logic alone is enough.

The living systems metaphor also has its limitations: it underplays the importance of intention. Organisations do not just respond to natural forces; they are made up of people who make choices and consciously decide what future they want for themselves. As Gareth Morgan points out, the living systems metaphor rests on the assumption of functional unity: each element of the system supporting and aiding the others, as in the human body. In organisations elements often do not support each other and can indeed conflict or break away from one another.

The two pictures do not come ideology free. The mechanical model is linked to the view that control is paramount and that senior managers do the thinking while others implement; the living systems thinking is associated with the assumption that organisations flourish as they allow their people to develop their potential to the full.

For us the challenge is not to adjudicate between these two conflicting pictures, nor to decide one is right and the other wrong, but rather to try and go deeper, to consider what each model offers, and then to integrate an approach to change which goes beyond both pictures while combining the best from both metaphors.

An example of this process of thinking is the business of quality. When quality was equated with luxury, people in business felt there was a choice: base your strategy on lower cost *or* higher quality. To add features to a product or service was to add cost. To lower cost would (usually) reduce the quality. Then along came the Japanese, redefining quality as reliability, consistency, products and services that kept their promise, whatever that was. Now a small car could be as much a quality product as a Rolls Royce. And suddenly lower costs went hand in hand with higher quality. Less waste in the factory meant lower production costs and greater product consistency. Increased cooperation between departments and reduced product development times meant lower costs and increased responsiveness to the customer.

The trick is in finding how to achieve the *ands*: how to combine the positive sides of apparently very different perspectives. By this we do not mean a compromise between the two views or a middle point. Rather we mean reframing the issues in a way that goes beyond the original perspectives, incorporating their benefits and finding a more rewarding picture of reality.

This is what we seek in this book: to go beyond the mechanical and living systems views of change and develop a practical guide for people in organisations. Both metaphors are very influential and widely used: people have found that they help them make sense of change. Our purpose therefore is not to knock them down, but to learn from them and to reframe the way we all consider change.

Leading *and* learning

The key value of the mechanical metaphor is the emphasis it places on *leading*. Effective leaders have a strong sense of intention and are clear, emotionally and logically, about what they want to change. They are true to their convictions and determined to see certain objectives and standards attained.

The key value of the living systems model is its focus on *learning*. It is not possible to prescribe in advance or in detail how people in an organisation will change and what shifts in thinking and behaviour will be required. The unpredictable always happens, so flexibility is essential. Leaders are learning along with everyone else in the organisation.

'Leaning into the future' recognises that effective leadership of change involves bringing together apparently contradictory qualities. Successful leaders shape the future *and* they adapt to the world as it is. They are clear about what they want to change *and* they are responsive to others' views and concerns. They are passionate about the direction in which they want the organisation to go *and* they understand and value the current reality of the organisation, why it has been successful and what its people are good at. They lead *and* they learn.

The image of a person leaning forward captures our view. To lean as far forward as you can requires you to have both feet firmly on the ground – stand on tip toe and you topple over.

What is intriguing is the power of the combination, of the *ands*. Far from being contradictory, the firm grasp on reality and the clear vision go hand in hand. The visions of leaders are clearer and more powerful if they have a firm grasp on reality. The clearer they are about what they want, the more they are able to get in touch with current reality.

Similarly and paradoxically, by recognising the limits of what they can do, they become more effective. They don't challenge the impossible but focus their efforts where they can succeed.

In the next chapter we explore how effective leaders ally leading *and* learning. How do they combine a fierce ambition to create the organisation they want with responsiveness to circumstances and to others' views and feelings? How do leaders shape the future *and* adapt to it?

In later chapters, we examine how individuals who combine leading and learning are able to:

❖ Develop 'seeing clearly', the shared understanding of current reality and possibilities as the stimulus for change
❖ 'Work with the grain' of their organisations, driving for the change they want and making the most of circumstances
❖ Recognise the need for 'all change', encouraging others to change by showing that they too are shifting
❖ 'Learn while doing', combining action and reflection to change the way their organisations work

4

Forthright *and* Listening Leadership

In a conversation with a client for whom we have the highest regard Colin said:

> *'You are demonstrating your ability to lead from the back again Gerry!'*

As he said it he realised that this phrase did not sound very complimentary, nor did it capture the essence of what he was trying to say. It was, however, said instinctively – so what did he mean?

Gerry's leadership style is very effective and it is different from the popular image of the leader on a white charger, blazing out in front of the troops, showing where to go and how to get there. The assumptions underpinning what we will call the white charger style of leadership are that people are impressed, stimulated and motivated to follow at great speed on the heels of such an inspirational leader. The role of the leader, in short, is to create the future and lead people to it. He or she (usually he in this model) has broad shoulders, vast amounts of vision, unerring judgment and a steady hand. In many ways a seductive model, but one which is frequently flawed.

The style of leadership which Gerry was demonstrating in this critical meeting was to make his own position very clear in terms of how he thought his new management team should function. He made his position equally clear on what he saw as the key issues in the business to address and some thoughts on how to go about addressing them. He then created an enormous amount of space and time for the other members of the team to outline their individual perspectives on these issues. The ensuing discussions were vigorous and healthy, the tone having been set (not just in that particular meeting) by Gerry's openness and willingness to be 'straight'. At the end of the meeting the team had not built a picture of the ideal organisation five years down the track, they even had different views of what it would look like. They did, however, have a much better understanding of each other and a high level of agreement on the short- and medium-term objectives. They were also crystal clear both about priorities and the way they were going to work to achieve them.

Gerry was using his unique blend of leadership skills to create the conditions for his team to lean into the future. He was as explicit as possible on key issues of direction, he was behaving and communicating in a 'straight', forthright manner. This encouraged the team members to pick up initiative, to challenge and to take action. As things progressed their insights and learning were fed into the overall direction and plans of the organisation.

CHARACTERISTICS OF LEADERS

What we are describing here are not the characteristics of 'the leader' (as in chief executive) in these organisations but of 'leading', something done by many people in all sorts of places in any company or organisation.

The leaders we have met demonstrate an authenticity which is clear to see for those who work with them. The message they are giving is obviously not a 'party line' or something which seems expedient at a given time. This allows them to communicate a genuineness to which people respond. It also enables them to be completely consistent in what they say and what they do.

They have sufficient personal confidence to lead at the same time as listening and to be challenged without feeling personally threatened. They also have a sense of how things should be different, a view of what they are aiming for, a sense of direction which creates space, and they allow freedom for people to pick initiative and get on with things.

Together we describe these qualities as *leading* and *learning*. This combination of opposites – leading as in 'from the front', from a confident, 'knowing' position, and learning as in willing to put themselves in question, open to challenge and new ideas from any source – is very much a part of, as opposed to above, the change process. These are leaders who *lean into the future*.

These leaders share a number of specific characteristics:

❖ Operational credibility
❖ Being 'connected' to their organisations
❖ Leading by example
❖ Consistency under pressure

Operational credibility

Contrary to some current theories of leadership which suggest that a good leader can lead any organisation through having interpersonal skills and financial acumen, the organisations we know mainly have leaders who are firmly rooted in a particular environment. They eat and sleep it, they can feel the products, understand the practical issues and difficulties, relate to the people – they are seen as operationally credible.

This is important for two reasons. They have the self-confidence to press ahead with change in operational areas and challenge existing ways of doing things. They can call on their own understanding and intuition to supplement information or put it into context. Secondly, they carry great weight with the operational managers they are working with to change. They are not seen as peddling textbook theories.

When Booker Farming Ltd, a subsidiary of the Booker Group, decided to use total quality management principles to develop its business, Managing Director Malcolm McAllister was aware that Booker Farming was somewhat different from many of the companies which had already worked with the concepts. With this in mind he, and his team of directors, spent time thinking through how the principles would apply 'down to the tractor seat'. This investment allowed them to communicate effectively to the whole organisation what total quality meant, in a concrete sense, to people at all levels.

He was equally aware that many employees were anxious about the initiative, seeing it as 'cost cutting under a new name', with jobs and longstanding traditions being threatened. To minimise anxiety and make the adoption of the methodologies as easy as possible, a series of workshops was held for all the farm managers. During these workshops the managers developed their understanding of total quality and aired their concerns and worries as they developed individual farm plans. Implementation was supported by the appointment of a senior farm manager as full-time total quality coordinator providing travelling support to all the farms. This served two purposes: first, it demonstrated the directors' commitment to the principles, and secondly, because of the farming experience and caring nature of the coordinator appointed, farm managers and employees believed that the values espoused in the approach were being lived out in reality.

Being 'connected' to their organisations

The leaders we have studied seem to have an intuitive connection to their organisation and industry which has been developed over years.

They also stay closely in touch with what is going on in the organisation.

In holiday company Club Med leaders at all levels work hard at keeping in touch both with their customers and their employees. A number of different examples show how this happens. During a period where significant amounts of time and effort were being put into quality improvement, Chief Executive Serge Trigano spent half a day every week with the team leading the quality improvement initiative. When it became apparent from trends in customer feedback that there was a need to change the layout of the restaurants to meet evolving customer expectations, the response was clear. He and his financial team took on-the-spot decisions about capital expenditure, agreeing to change all the restaurants over a three-year period starting the following year. This sent clear signals to the organisation about the importance of customer feedback and the willingness of the chief executive to take decisions based on it.

Leadership in Club Med is about the amount of time spent by Village Managers 'on the ground' being out and about with GMs (*gentils membres* – holiday makers) and GOs (*gentils organisateurs* – staff). At another level, Francis di Landro, an experienced Village Manager, shows how he keeps in touch with the customers and models what is required of employees. He says, 'If the GOs see me talking to GMs, they will talk to GMs; if they see me checking the standards, they will check the standards; if I am approachable, they will be approachable.' While running a business which has (at any one time) up to 1000 guests and 400 staff, with all the budgeting, planning and organising that requires, the manager would still spend seven to eight hours a day 'on the ground' with the guests and staff.

Another area of leadership by example in Club Med is the *retour au source* programme whereby all managers working at head office spend a month each year working as GOs in a village. This is an enormously powerful process for a number of reasons. First, it shows all the GOs that senior managers believe the job is important enough for them to spend a month doing it. Secondly, it keeps senior managers directly in touch with the GMs where otherwise they might become remote.

Thirdly, as nearly all the senior managers were GOs themselves they have a wealth of experience and Club 'spirit' to bring to any village they go and work in. Fourthly, it is cost effective, getting people out to the 'sharp end' when it is busiest at a time when Head Office is relatively quiet.

Leading by example

People don't believe bullshit!

The greatest single influencing factor in any change process is the example set by people who command respect and have influence. There is a rule of thumb which says 'employees judge a manager's commitment to any change 10 per cent on what he or she says and 90 per cent on what he or she does'. If leaders practise the approach 'Do as I say, not as I do!', they are guaranteed to fail in achieving the change in philosophy or way of working they are seeking.

This is why leadership by example is so critical. Part of the issue is the leader's willingness to scrutinise their own behaviour as hard as they do that of other people. What direct impact are they having with the behaviour they are modelling? This is particularly true when the leaders are under pressure.

The behaviour of leaders under pressure provides insights into their underlying beliefs and commitment. It also highlights the underlying patterns of individual behaviour, as we tend to 'revert to type' when we feel under pressure. Staff look for critical incidents as a guide for where the leader's real commitment lies. What is the reaction when a mistake is made, when a deadline is drawing very near or when a decision is being challenged? Does the manager continue to display the same behaviour or do they revert to the style of management which was previously the normal way? These occasions require nerve and a steady hand on the part of managers. As Peter Wickens, previously Director of Personnel and Information Systems at Nissan UK, says, 'To achieve real quality everyone in the organisation has to genuinely believe it and act on the belief. Management must mean what it says. As soon as a senior manager lets a car go through which is not the right quality level "because I have to meet the schedule" the battle is lost.'

In the light of this evidence there is a clear argument for saying very little, making few promises of a bright new future and just getting on with being different. Marketing people have known for years that over-promising is a fatal mistake, as customer disappointment comes hard behind. Leaders involved in change must learn the same lesson. Visible differences in behaviour are noticed, if they continue they are copied and so change occurs.

This sounds very easy and to a certain extent it is. Sometimes it is necessary just to get on with it. However, there is one essential ingredient and that, as an experienced manager put it to us, is courage. Leaders have to have the courage to take risks, to experiment, to encourage others to experiment and to support them if things get difficult. It is much easier, in the short term, not to do this. It is also critical to develop an understanding of what is really stopping change happening. What are the blockages and bottlenecks? These are often generalised into 'fear of change'. It is a key role of the leader to provide time, patience and some skill to surface and share underlying assumptions and concerns about how things are at the moment and why they are as they are.

The old adage 'do as you would be done by' provides a clear, simple, relevant message for leaders seeking to bring about change in organisations. Behaviour is learnt. This learnt behaviour can be changed if individuals feel that the change will in some way make them feel better about themselves and how they relate to others. People being asked to change are under some stress. They may not admit it, even to themselves, but the implicit message behind a request for change is that the way they have done things in the past (which may well have led them to be successful) is no longer right, appropriate or good enough. Under stress we become potentially more suspicious of new things, less open, less able to adapt, so we resist change.

Modelling the required behaviours, consistently, becomes essential under these circumstances. If openness and support are required then openness and support should be provided in the process of change, even though this may be uncomfortable to the leaders of change as they themselves are part of it and feel under some stress too. This really is the role of leadership. Consistent, visible behaviour sends powerful signals around the organisation and has a greater effect than 'glossy' visions. By the same token, behaviour which reinforces existing patterns will be equally clearly seen and will result in undesired reinforcement of the *status quo*. Creating a climate of self-confidence in which individuals feel encouraged and able to change is essential.

Consistent under pressure

An excellent example of consistent behaviour under pressure is that of the management team at the Chantiers de l'Atlantique, the French ship-yard owned by GEC ALSTHOM on the Loire at St Nazaire. Nine years ago the management of the shipyard stopped, reflected and thought long and hard about how they had contributed to the poor labour relations position which had developed. They were prepared to be self-critical, to challenge their own assumptions about how to run the business and to experiment, to take some risks. In the absence of information a labyrinth of networks and grapevines had developed, most of which were either wrong in the information they carried or wildly exaggerated. The managers decided that much more open and honest, two-way communication was needed between the senior man-agement and the people actually building the ships.

Every Wednesday there is now a cascade briefing process which gets directly to all 5000 staff within five hours of issues being discussed at the weekly management committee meeting first thing on Wednesday morning. As Michel Pommies, the Production Director, says: 'We have replaced the grapevine because over a number of years our information has proved to be more accurate and more reliable'. This formal process, known within the shipyard as *la messe du Mercredi* (Wednesday mass), is complemented by other activities which clearly demonstrate manage-ment's desire to be open. Both the speed with which it is done and the genuine motivation to be more open mean that this team briefing works well (many don't!) as part of an overall management process.

Another demonstration of this commitment to open communication is the production director's meetings with his staff. He holds face-to-face discussions with each member of his staff at least once every six months by conducting two-hour meetings with 100 people at a time. Any questions are taken and answered as well as possible. Given that 4000 of the 5000 employees report to him, this means the meetings are a weekly event. On being challenged by his peers at a management seminar of the GEC ALSTHOM group about the amount of his time this used, he returned the question and asked, 'How can you make better use of your time?'

Introduced in a concerted effort to change the conflictual nature of the relationship between management and employees, over the five years that this system of communications has been in place labour relations have improved dramatically. It was not easy initially: employees were cynical and the union openly hostile, seeing the system as a move to weaken its own direct information supply to the workforce. As Michel Pommies explains:

My desk was thrown out through the office window early on. The questions were direct and tough but we kept going and gradually things improved. It is difficult to see how we could run the business without it now. We tell things as they are, good news and bad. There are some things we cannot divulge at any given point in time (for example commercially sensitive information) but we keep them as few as possible and people respect the fact we are being as open as we feel we possibly can be.

The success of such a process comes as much from this example, this honesty and commitment, as from the tool or technique employed. The result is that the same team of managers is now running one of the most successful shipbuilding businesses in the world, in an industry in which most European enterprises have failed to meet the global challenges.

Leading in change

The ability to *lean into the future* can be resumed in two apparent paradoxes. First, the ability of leaders to provide a clear sense of *direction*, combined with an enthusiasm for giving people *autonomy* to think and act. Second, their willingness to be *forthright* in action and communication and to *listen* hard and effectively to what is happening inside, and outside, their organisation. How well leaders live these paradoxes will largely determine their organisation's ability to work in change.

Intriguingly, the qualities found at opposing ends of each paradox can be complementary not contradictory, they support and reinforce each other. Providing a clear sense of direction enables people to pick up responsibility, to get on and take initiative. Equally, where leaders are true to themselves and state with feeling the things they believe in, this provides the environment in which others can present their views and feelings, honestly and directly. We often encounter leaders who hold back for fear that their views will crowd out those of others. In our experience the reverse is true. If leaders 'own' their views, don't impose them on others but simply make clear what is really important to them, this can be an enormous relief to other people and enable them to be equally straightforward and clear in presenting what matters to them.

PARADOX 1 – FORTHRIGHT *AND* LISTENING

Forthright leadership

The leaders we spoke to are frank and direct. They are prepared to 'go out on a limb' for the things they believe in. They will not be bound by convention, longstanding practices or unnecessary bureaucracy. This often involves taking personal risk with their reputations and careers.

They are not however outspoken, 'loud', rash or irresponsible. They lead by example and expect others to do the same.

Howard Selland, President of Aeroquip, the American-owned, international supplier of components to the automotive, industrial and aerospace industries, demonstrates enormous personal commitment to the issues he feels are critical to the future of the company. Examples of this are the huge product and process rationalisation programme launched in 1991, the establishment of a centre of technological leadership with a brief to 'develop the products of the next century', creating Aeroquip's own quality framework (derived from the Baldrige framework) and demanding that the different operating units reach the standards established within an agreed time frame. How they do it is up to each unit, but the standards are non-negotiable.

Howard is not impressed by neatly sculptured strategic plans and documents, believing that these often bear little relationship to what is actually happening in a business. He pushes his various management teams' strategic thinking and capability in a way which directly influences what gets done. This is realised through regular visits to divisions and operating units and engaging in vigorous debates with the management teams about what he sees as important, what they see as important and what the differences are. At the end of these meetings no one is in any doubt as to what Howard thinks and believes about the issues debated! At a 1994 meeting with the International Division he was completely uncompromising about the need to focus the business around perceived value by selected customer clusters. How the senior managers in the division go about doing this was largely down to them. As he says, 'The local teams have to run their businesses, I am not here to tell them how to do it. But I do have some strong views on what we should be doing. They have to hear me, I want to hear them and then they work out how to proceed.'

In ICL David Palk, General Manager of Product Distribution, inherited an operation 'in a mess'. As a 28 year old he only got the job because older, 'wiser' men thought the post too risky. He flouted corporate policies when it was necessary to get things done for customers, provoking howls of protest from both the corporate quality and financial staff. He harried and pushed on the detail of what happened on each individual shipment until people got the message that customers were all that mattered.

The message was reinforced by action. Every day David sat down at 4 pm with his team of 20 managers and went through individual part numbers on the computer printout, checking whether items were on time and what was being done to remedy any problems. Soon the view which staff had of current reality shifted. Instead of feeling doomed to poor performance and decline, they began to see that an unremitting focus on customer service could produce results and could save the unit. Instead of feeling powerless, they began to see what they could do. The results followed. From a record in 1988 of 27 per cent of complete orders delivered when promised to the customer, the unit moved to achieving near 100 per cent performance.

It is important to note that forthright does not automatically mean clear. Sometimes leaders cannot be clear, because they just don't know, they are as confused as everyone else! Traditionally leaders have tried to hide this. They believe that they mustn't show weakness or doubt. Given that one of the vital elements of organisations leaning into the future is that everyone takes greater responsibility for themselves and for the whole, this approach is no longer valid. Demonstrating fallibility enables others to pick up responsibility. Being forthright about what they are thinking or feeling may not come naturally to some leaders (or comfortably at first to those they are leading) but it forces responsibility down and improves the organisation's ability to respond.

Listening, responsive leadership

Many of the organisations we know do not have charismatic leaders. For learning and development to take place leaders have to give employees space to work things out for themselves, to make mistakes, to review and learn from what they have done. The leaders, while insistent on standards and objectives, seek to involve others in working out how to achieve objectives. They are usually modest, sometimes even self-effacing, losing no opportunity to stress that real achievement has come from teamwork, not the inspiration of just one individual. They face problems when they don't know all the answers and they look for support from anyone around to solve them. Not pretending to be the source of all wisdom, demonstrating some fallibility, is a powerful way of developing commitment to and ownership of issues by others.

An example of this is the Japanese managers who worked with the start-up team in Nissan UK. Despite their vastly superior record in running car businesses they did not come to the UK to tell the British managers how to do it. They questioned, they challenged, they drove the British managers wild at times with their examination of the accepted way of doing things and their attention to detail; but they made it plain from the start that the decisions and the responsibility for running a British plant with British workers rested with British management. This style is born out by the British management team. They are softly spoken, questioning, listening, not status conscious and more likely to say 'we' than 'I'.

In Grundfos, the Danish-owned water pump manufacturer with a 50 per cent world market share, leadership is not based on personality but on consistent, meaningful support. Finn Moller, who led a fundamental change in their way of operating in the factory to remove most checking and inspection from the production line, says, 'The most important thing top management did was supporting me even when they disagreed with what I was doing.' Moral support, making money or people's time available, space to make progress without being obsessed with this month's operational results: this is what encouraged people and enabled them to keep going when things were difficult.

The extent to which listening is underestimated as a crucial aspect of leading is highlighted in the following lines from Peter Hawkins' forthcoming book *Consult the Wise Fool: Mulla Nasrudin becomes a Management Consultant*:

A corporate senior management team asked the Mulla whether or not he could prepare a communications policy for them, so that they could communicate better with their 6000 staff. 'Certainly', said the Mulla, 'only first tell me, in communicating with your staff, what is it that you are not hearing?'

It is the combination of forthrightness *and* listening which is powerful. One recent case illustrated how forthrightness was the precondition to listening. A managing director we worked with was keen to draw his management team into genuine debate about his company's strategy. He was frustrated because he felt that when the team reviewed strategy most of his subordinates held back. On many key issues they refused to engage with him. Having experienced this difficulty, he was determined in a workshop we facilitated to hold back on his contributions and allow others space, as he saw it, to put in their views. The approach didn't work. The subordinates said less of real substance than ever and overall the discussion was superficial. The breakthrough to a more challenging and incisive debate occurred when we persuaded the MD to disclose more of his personal views. By declaring his hand, saying 'where he was coming from' but doing so in a way that he 'owned' his views and did not impose them on others, he freed the others to speak out. By being forthright in his opinions, he encouraged them to be forthright and state views to which he could then listen.

PARADOX 2 – DIRECTION *AND* AUTONOMY

The leaders described demonstrate the characteristics of being forthright and listening. However, to understand better how they are effective it is also necessary to look at their ability to create the context and environment within which they and other people operate: how they provide direction and encourage autonomy.

Direction

Most leaders recognise the need for a sense of direction. They see it as an integral part of their role to provide this. In some cases they see it as entirely their responsibility, in others there is a preference for a more involving, collegiate approach to developing direction.

BSG International is a group manufacturing and marketing components for the automotive and aircraft industries, supplying child safety equipment and furniture and running a vehicle distribution and leasing business, with a group turnover of £500 million. When Richard Marton became its Chief Executive, he stated explicitly that he was going to involve people far more than had previously been the case in the development of the new group strategy, and that this team approach was something he wished to encourage across the group. As the strategy development process unfolded, each of the directors was encouraged to represent the views of his division *and* to act as a group director, being forthright and candid in all the discussions.

Richard's vision of what the group should do was not fundamentally changed during this process, but the clarity of the portfolio of businesses and the understanding of the group's 'core competences', what they were really good at, meant that divisional and company managing directors could go ahead, make and implement decisions in alignment with the overall direction.

This kind of clarity can be sought anywhere in an organisation: it is equally important for a department, function or process leader to seek to provide clarity of direction. Importantly, the direction does not have to be the definitive, immutable direction – it has to be the best at the time, as clear as is possible and up for regular review.

Autonomy

Greater clarity enables greater autonomy. Leaders can build on the direction they provide by giving people space, time and knowledge to take initiative. This is commonly translated as 'empowerment'. Widely talked of, this has become one of the most used and abused management concepts of the last decade. Most managers talk freely of empowerment, but how many have defined what they mean?

We dislike the word empowerment, which is in any event misleading (you can disempower somebody but you cannot empower them: a sense of power, if it is to mean anything, must come from within, at the wish of the person concerned). In order to allow people to realise their true potential, leaders 'enable' people to take the initiative: by being as clear as they can on direction and principles, providing the necessary guidance for people to be self-starting.

The phrase 'freedom within a framework' was invented by a group of managers working in Norwich Union to try and communicate what they felt was an appropriate way of enabling people to feel empowered. Many organisations have struggled with the concept of empowerment. This was a way of making it more accessible, more meaningful to people by providing clear boundaries within which they can experiment. The framework in this case included specific policy guidelines, behavioural norms around the acceptability of mistakes, where it was OK to experiment (and where it was not), the right to challenge and issues of reward and recognition.

People will really begin to change, take initiative, take risks, provide real feedback, learn from mistakes and accept responsibility for what they are doing when they feel sufficiently confident to do so and are provided with a clear framework. This requires them to have a different type of relationship with their managers to that of the traditional 'squaddie to sergeant'. The employee must feel able both to challenge and support, to work independently of the manager and in close collaboration with them.

Achieving this type of relationship is not easy. It requires much effort, openness and willingness to learn – and some humility. It feels uncomfortable, particularly for leaders in organisations where this style is not the norm. It requires a high degree of self-belief and a willingness to try.

Again it is the *combination* which is most effective: allying clear direction with scope for autonomy. In one company, for example, more directive behaviour by directors provided the framework within which staff could take advantage of autonomy. The directors had set up some project teams to look at a series of key business issues. The teams were multi-functional and multi-level, including people from the shopfloor alongside senior managers. This way of addressing issues was a new departure for the company, which had a very 'top-down' style of management. Ironically, when it came to setting up the teams senior management did not give enough direction. They were concerned to give the teams 'room' in which they could challenge existing ways of operating and think radically about what the company needed. They stood well back, did not give the teams clear objectives or an adequate definition of the scope of issues they could look at. Nor did the senior managers advise on important implementation issues. The result was that the teams floundered initially and wasted time. Without clear boundaries to work within they found it very hard to get going and focus on what they could do. It was only after a review, when senior managers saw the need to give the teams clearer parameters within which to work, that the teams began to be successful.

LEANING INTO THE FUTURE

The opportunity for successful leaders is to combine these two paradoxes in a way which provides coherent leadership to the people who work with them.

The framework in Figure 4.1 demonstrates how leaders can integrate these paradoxes in an operational leadership model. It is cyclical, showing a sequence of activities as well as style preferences or 'comfort zones' for individuals. There is no start or finish, but there is a cycle to be completed and counterbalancing forces.

For example, if a leader gives a clear sense of direction, perhaps in the form of plans and goals (Step 1) and communicates forthrightly (Step 2), he or she is creating the space for people to take initiative, to act

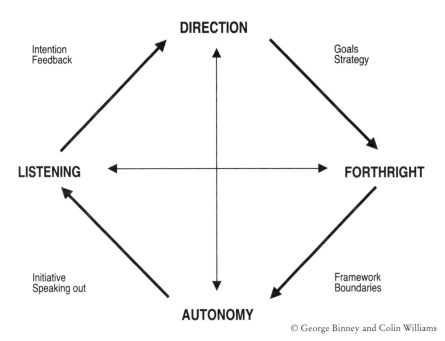

Figure 4.1 Combining the paradoxes

autonomously (Step 3) within the guiding principles. This is genuine empowerment: people feel a sense of power. This thinking and action open up lines of enquiry as people explore possibilities and problems. At this point the leader needs to be listening attentively (Step 4) in order to pick up vital signals, to keep in touch with the organisation because a process of discovery is occurring. The leader can then use the discovery, the new insights and understanding to inform and revise the direction (Step 1). In this way the organisation is learning and adapting constantly.

As people work round the cycle, it is important to think about what is involved in each step and what will complement later steps in the cycle. Chris Argyris and Donald Schon have highlighted the risks of manipulation, of managers appearing to be sensitive to the opinions of others but actually having minds that are already made up: 'All manner of skills may be employed, "listening with rapt attention", "invitations to participate" but actually the manager's purpose is to sell his/her original conviction.' The lack of openness may also be connected to a sincere desire to avoid hurting the feelings of others, but the damage is done all the same: 'You cannot learn to perform better if managers are too squeamish to contrast a mediocre performance with a higher standard.'

What the model draws attention to is the need for genuine openness, advocating positions in a forthright way and being prepared to change what is advocated in a shared exploration for a better solution. The listening we describe is not a passive activity but an energetic attention to all the available signals and information, all the data that may help in discovering the better answer.

Similarly, the direction we are describing sets frameworks and boundaries in which others can work effectively: it is not a stifling direction which leaves no scope for others, but a liberating approach.

By working round the cycle, leaders combine forthrightness and listening, direction and autonomy, and it is these combinations which are powerful.

This model can be used in a number of different ways:

* ❖ By the individual leader to identify where their own natural preferences lie, both in terms of what they are good at/not good at, do/don't do and to identify which steps in the cycle they are likely either to miss out or do too much of
* ❖ By teams to plot their profiles against each other to try and understand sources of difference and difficulty. It can provide a vehicle for raising the shared understanding of working with change, to discuss differences in a way which reduces direct criticism and personal attack
* ❖ By people leading change to consider how they should plan an initiative or project which involves major change

THE CHANGING NATURE OF LEADERSHIP

Often people leading in change find themselves facing the need for quite a significant shift in the way things are done. This does not happen overnight, but if it is to happen at all a number of assumptions that leaders hold about their role and purpose need to be brought to the surface and worked through. One of the most fundamental of these is the nature of the relationship between manager and employee. At the heart of this relationship are power and control.

Much of what we cover in this chapter does not describe the leaders of many successful organisations. What of the autocrats, you may be thinking? How do we account for the captains of industry who run huge companies by personally making every important decision, by making it their business to know what is going on everywhere and by firing people who disagree with them?

We do not (indeed could not) suggest that they are not successful: there are many ways to manage. However, we do make two comments.

First, there is always a price to pay for riding roughshod over people. Compliance can be demanded but commitment cannot. People will give grudgingly what they have to, not all that they can. The price for this is usually paid in the long term, and often not noticed, such has been the euphoria over the short-term gains.

Second, the world is changing. What was successful in organisations created along scientific principles, the machine analogy again, will no longer be successful in the future. It is one of the ironies of today that although more and more people are unemployed, there is a constant lament that 'good people' are hard to find for key jobs. Surely the organisations which lament the shortage of good people should recognise their responsibility in developing them. In reality, 'good people' are making choices about who they want to work for and what kind of rewards they are seeking. In order to recruit, develop and retain the best people leaders will have to look at what these people want out of work – and autonomy is high on most people's list. Autocratic leadership is no longer appropriate.

The paradox for leaders is that as they give away power, so they become more powerful! People within organisations feel more responsible, more committed and their energy and creativity increase. Individuals who take greater responsibility for themselves and for the work they do are nearly always more satisfied with their job and more fulfilled as people.

As organisations lean into the future the role of leaders as guides, as enablers, as models and as people who will provide challenge and support is critical.

FORTHRIGHT AND LISTENING LEADERSHIP: THE EUROPEAN PATENT OFFICE

The European Patent Office (EPO) was created in 1977 out of its predecessor the IIB. Its purpose is to research patent applications and issue patents to European industry and other industrial organisations wishing to sell products into EU member states. It is run by an administrative council on which sit representatives of the national patent offices of the member countries, with whom the EPO also competes for business under some circumstances.

To meet the requirements of the interested parties who created it, it is located in three different geographic locations: a large office in The Hague, DG1 (1700 people approximately), a large office in Munich (about 1500 people) and a much smaller office in Berlin (about 100 people). There is also a small patent information office (100 people) in Vienna. This particular case study is based on DG1, which is responsible for patent searches.

The vice president in charge of DG1, Jacques Michel, recognised a number of years ago that the external context within which the 'Office' was operating was changing rapidly. The changes included a greater requirement from customers for price competitivity; the possibility of a worldwide patent emerging; a revolution in information management having an impact on their core competence; and a political context which was becoming increasingly difficult to predict.

He contrasted this external situation with the internal context of DG1. DG1 was perceived by its customers to be doing high-quality search work, albeit at too high a cost. The internal climate was bureaucratic, some would say rigid, with well-established practices and procedures dominating what was done and how it was done. These working practices were both expensive and restrictive, their inflexibility making any sort of experimentation and innovation difficult to achieve. Jacques Michel saw that the longer-term future of the Office was in danger unless some fundamental changes in how it operated were achieved.

The office has a number of distinctive characteristics:

❖ *The vast majority of its employees are drawn from the various European member countries. They have expatriate status and are not subject to local employment legislation*
❖ *The majority of employees are highly qualified (PhD-level) scientists and engineers, many recognised as leaders in their fields.*
❖ *The nature of the work has traditionally required people to work in isolation, doing patent information searches, on-line computer searches, making judgements and writing reports.*

Together these create a fairly special atmosphere with a strong internal focus, a degree of 'comfort' (being protected to a certain extent by unique status) and a belief that professionalism will win in the end (we are so good people will always want to do business with us).

One of the first activities Jacques Michel undertook was to raise senior staff's awareness of the changing external environment. This was achieved using a number of means, one of the most significant being a seminar led by Herve Sérieyx, a leading French thinker on the future of organisations and management. Following this event an internal working party was created, 'the change group', to think about how to accelerate the pace of change within the Office. Some of the activities which were undertaken before and during this period were:

❖ a number of teams were established to experiment with IT-based information documentation, storage and retrieval
❖ teams were set up to experiment with integrating search and patent-issuing activities (which historically had been distinct)
❖ the entire organisation was restructured, from having one 'central services' organisation providing administrative support to 40 groups of search examiners. 'Clusters' were set up of four groups of search examiners (each of about 25 examiners) with about 25 administrative staff. The aim was to create units which were small enough to have some identity and generate a sense of belonging for members, yet large enough to have some real authority and responsibility delegated to them
❖ a process was put in place to shift accountabilities from purely individual to team-based performance

Jacques Michel's role in this process was absolutely critical. As a highly qualified and experienced research scientist (he was previously Director of the Documentation Centre of the CNRS, Centre National de Recherches Scientifiques, in Paris), he commanded the intellectual respect of the members of his organisation. He combined this with the leadership characteristics and approach described in this chapter.

He understood the need for change and had a clear idea of some of the things which needed to change. He could not, however, be explicit about the direction the organisation needed to take. He stated openly that the future was not clear, that they could not make concrete plans for the next five years with firm objectives and milestones. He expressed this view frequently and firmly to as many people as possible. The message was not always well received. One examiner challenged him, saying, 'You tell us we have to change but you are not telling us what we have to change to.' He replied by outlining the situation as clearly as he could, finishing with, 'It is impossible for me to predict the future any more specifically than this. I am not God!'

Jacques Michel is very willing to 'push and prod', to ask awkward questions and make unpopular decisions where necessary. Equally, he listens attentively to what people say, seeking to incorporate their ideas into the way forward. This is particularly so when they are trying to convert a principle (e.g. devolving authority) into practice (by allowing different directors to start with different issues). He is keen to provide space for others to experiment and will support them through difficulties. He is equally comfortable participating enthusiastically in an open discussion about the nature of management in the Office with staff members, sharing jokes and ideas in a relaxed way, as he is arguing determinedly with key players in the external political environment.

Perhaps most importantly, he is very clear that he alone cannot make the changes needed in the European Patent Office. The success of the changes and the future of the Office are dependent on other people, the people who work in the Office, 'owning the future' and working through a number of fundamental changes. He sees his role as to helping them pick up that ownership, creating the context, providing the support, encouragement and self-belief for it to happen.

The European Patent Office in The Hague is in the process of a major change. A number of differences are clearly obvious to people who knew it three years ago. There is a greater responsiveness to new ideas, a willingness to experiment, and people are picking up responsibility for actions outside their specific job accountabilities. A process of learning and transferring of ideas is flourishing. The increase in energy is almost tangible. The next few years should see a continuing growth in this direction.

5

Seeing Clearly

In Chapter 2 we are critical of the current spate of 'vision-led' change initiatives because they rely on a utopian dream or idealised future state to provide the energy for change, and ignore the need for discovering a shared understanding of current reality and for identifying choice as the source of energy for change. Vision has become so much a part of how people think about change that to take it away would seem like removing the road map from a driver in an unknown country. Yet this overdependence on vision is at the root of many failed change initiatives. It is too logical, too neat: it suggests a degree of certainty and predictability which creates a false sense of security and causes people leading in change to lose focus and allow energy to be wasted.

Central to the thinking about change we outline in this book is the observation that processes of change start with focusing on current reality – rather than describing a desired future state. This is in part a pragmatic view. Too many efforts start by trying to formulate clear visions of the future and end in generalities and 'management speak'.

The vision statements neither inspire nor impress. They don't connect with the reality people know. They often seem to denigrate the past and they are not matched by management action and behaviour that would make them credible.

However, a sense of direction is important, so how can this be achieved? Vision defined as 'the sense of seeing clearly', vision which emerges in the process of doing and of understanding more of 'what is', can help change. This sort of vision is rooted in the experience of the organisation. It does not come from management 'awaydays' alone, nor from writing down aspirations, however eloquent. It is, as Henry Mintzberg describes, an 'integrated perspective of the organization, a not too precisely articulated vision of direction'. It encapsulates the intention of people in the organisation about the change they want – but with due humility.

Vision versus reality

Starting with current reality is the foundation stone of an uncommon view of the way people in organisations change. Paradoxically the energy for change comes from becoming more aware of where the organisation is now. What is it like for staff to work in the organisation? How does work actually get done – not the theory laid out in the procedure manuals but the reality? What is the experience of customers, suppliers and others when dealing with the organisation? What is their perception – not what the organisation would like to believe but their real feelings and views? What do they value in what the organisation does? What is working and what is not? What are the real issues and obstacles that staff have to deal with? What prevents people giving of their best? What do people truly want to change? How are the demands of the company's environment changing?

Leaders need to ensure that this understanding of current reality is informed from a number of sources. Building a shared understanding about what is happening inside the organisation is fundamental, but equally important is the need for an unbiased, external perspective on the organisation and its relationship to its external environment. Together these perspectives can provide a powerful and 'rooted' sense of direction for the organisation. In the words of Marcel Proust, 'The real art of discovery consists not in finding new lands but in seeing with new eyes.' Leaders in change work effectively with their own view of direction which they allow to be informed and modified by the emerging clarity of what is really possible. In some organisations, once people are really engaged and excited the leader's initial goal or vision can seem unambitious!

We will look first at understanding the internal current reality, then explore the external perspective.

INTERNAL REALITY

The challenge for managers is to create the climate, the circumstances, the situations in which people can explore current reality. The inter-action which takes place when people openly explore issues is what identifies options and choices. People 'discover' a new reality in their organisation as a result of sharing their thoughts and feelings. This discovery creates choices and energy which are transformed into action.

What characterises organisations which seek to understand current reality, to review openly and honestly, to discover themselves and 'see with new eyes'?

Seeing and hearing things 'as they are'

Often people in organisations feel insulted by change initiatives which seem deaf to their concerns. One hospital in Britain's National Health Service introduced a change programme at the initiative of the chairman of the newly formed trust which ran the hospital. He came from the private industry sector and felt that change was urgently needed to make the hospital more responsive to its patients. The perception of people working in the hospital, however, was that their real concerns – about excessive workloads, poor pay and conditions, constant reorganisations – were ignored, and that a 'change agenda' was being imposed which bore no connection to the reality of their working lives. Because their concerns were interpreted as negative and symptomatic of a lack of commitment, staff paid lip-service at best to the new initiative and the programme gradually ran into the sand.

Very often we are struck by the gap in perception between those seeking to lead change and those they are seeking to influence. Even with the best of intentions senior managers can sometimes become disconnected from their operating business in a way which makes it difficult for them to see reality 'as it is'. The chief executive's desire to keep things moving and work through the important issues on the agenda for the business can make it very difficult for operating managers to tell them news about progress which is less rapid or less encouraging than they wish to hear.

In one leading food manufacturer we worked with the renowned impatience and belligerence of the chief executive had a number of unfortunate consequences which ultimately outweighed his energy and positive contribution to the company.

He found himself becoming more and more isolated from his business. For example, he discovered poor performance in parts of his business when financial reports came in: other senior managers knew earlier but were not prepared to risk telling him. Difficulties in inter-company trading were made known to him in front of his peers at a group board meeting: his own purchasing people could have briefed him, since they knew it was a problem long before the meeting.

Eventually the only two directors who were prepared to stand up to him moved on, leaving him isolated. His position became increasingly untenable and the company results were not good. He was transferred to another post within the group some months later.

Using simple and direct language

Closely linked to the hearing of things 'as they are' is the importance of using simple and direct language. Change efforts are bedevilled by 'management speak' and business school terminology. The reality of problems and opportunities is completely obscured by mind-numbing jargon. It's not just managers wanting to show they can use fashionable language: it goes to the heart of what people are about. Until clear, simple words are used, reality has not been clearly identified.

Simple, direct language has to be what people will recognise and understand. Some managers, in an effort to shift people's perceptions, have changed the language: 'passengers' on British Rail have become 'customers', as have some 'patients' in the National Health Service. The problem is that the ground work has not been done: staff have not agreed that a change of name is needed. Instead it is imposed. Often staff feel instinctively that 'customer' is not the right word: their passengers and patients are different from customers, and the reality of the relationships will always be different. Saying 'customer' is felt to demean the quality and distinctiveness of the service which staff have provided in the past and underestimate the richness of relationships in the future.

Quality, excellence, customer focus, learning, empowerment, continuous improvement, mission and vision: all these words have been debased. Managers have become so used to hearing and seeing them that they often feel obliged to include them in statements without being clear what they mean in the context of their organisation. The words are also often indicative of a lack of thinking, or at least they may show the paucity of thinking. The implicit assumption seems to be: 'we're not clear what we mean so we'll throw in a few buzzwords which will sound good.' When people are addressed in 'management speak' they quickly recognise the smoke screen.

The most powerful messages resonate instantly with people. A good test is to try statements out with people on the shopfloor or the customer contact points and ask if they make any sense to them: not because the understanding of people there is any less, but because they are not so used to management language and are more likely to say that the emperor has no clothes.

When David Palk assumed responsibility for the Literature and Software Distribution Operation of ICL in 1988, he used plain English to describe the challenge the organisation faced. The unit had a very poor service record, with a six-month backlog of work. He said out loud what many people were thinking: the unit was about to die. It had to be turned round or it would close. David didn't talk about quality or excellence – communicating to everyone he said: 'Everything is focused on customers; it's as simple as that.'

Drawing on new information and perspectives

Sometimes it is new information: more often it is information which was always there but never seen. A mirror can be held up to people in organisations in a way that shows their behaviour and actions in a very different light from the one they have been used to.

Grundfos, the remarkable Danish company, is an example. From its foundation in 1945 it has prided itself on superior product quality. Yet when Finn Moller, the current Quality Director, joined the company in 1981, he found a lack of proper procedures and systems. In the words of one manager, 'We were just one big blacksmith' with different approaches and standards, depending on who was doing the work. One of the first things Finn organised was a team which red-tagged all the raw materials and work in progress that did not meet the specifications. Suddenly mountains of red tags appeared all around the factory. Everyone could see that specifications and drawings were being routinely ignored. It was clear that if specifications were not followed to the letter or changed, the company's reputation for superb quality would be at risk. A process was started which over several years gave the company a systematic approach to delivering quality.

Valuing experience

The lessons from past successes and difficulties abound in all organisations if the space can be created to explore them and there is a willingness to look openly at them without seeking to blame and punish. In order to understand how and why things happen in a particular way it is necessary to draw out the views of a range of stakeholders. Each will have their own 'truth' and each is equally valid.

A common problem is that managers feel they don't want to 'get bogged down in detail'. Exploring in detail incidents from the past feels negative and unproductive. 'Let's be positive,' they say, 'let's talk about what we want to be in the future.' Our experience is the opposite. It is by dwelling on real-life incidents, understanding what lies behind them, the patterns of thinking and behaviour, that people come to a clearer understanding of reality and what they want to change – provided, of course, that it is done with a constructive intent.

In our work with primary care teams in a doctors' surgery, one group was in uproar over an incident that had happened at a meeting the week before. They felt very strongly about a moment when doctors had been challenged, by an outside facilitator, to offer an evening surgery which would be more convenient for patients. The doctors felt angry about being imposed on; nurses and others, on the other hand, were frankly delighted that the doctors had been directly challenged. In the course of the discussion one doctor asked what was the point of reviewing the incident: 'Let's be positive, let's move on,' he said. Yet the incident illustrated perfectly many of the challenges which the group faced: the pretend equality between doctors and others; the reluctance to confront uncomfortable issues; the lack of communication between different groups. By drawing out the patterns illustrated by the incident, the group was able to learn about itself, to see in the open problems which were constantly undermining its effectiveness and begin to see how to deal with them.

Central to open, honest review is a sense that the past is valued, that people feel that all the effort and hard work they have put in are appreciated and that the learning accumulated over time is recognised. One reason we are critical of reengineering and the other fads calling for constant upheaval in organisations is that they 'throw the baby out with the bath water'. By calling on organisations to 'start from a fresh sheet of paper', they ignore what people and organisations have done well in the past and need to carry into the future. They make what many in the field of business strategy now recognise as a cardinal error: they pretend that organisations can learn from scratch and quickly the distinctive competences that deliver value to customers (or other stakeholders). It is because these competences are 'baked' into organisations and cannot easily be copied by competitors that they enable organisations to earn a living. Increasingly strategists are pointing to the need for organisations to understand more about what they do well and build on it: not reinventing themselves but making the most of what they have and growing from it.

Often organisations do not see clearly what they do well. They are too close to it or they take for granted skills and aptitudes which others find very impressive. As well as objective external feedback, they need to make sense of the past. Looking inside and understanding why the organisation has been successful is an essential part of open, honest review.

Bringing to the surface the 'undiscussables'

All organisations have subjects and issues which everyone knows are not politically correct conversation material. Sometimes these subjects cause immense frustration and waste inordinate amounts of time and energy. These are things like apparently unfair management perks; measurement systems which measure the wrong things or give the information to the wrong people; 'turf' or boundary battles; the inability to express fear or concern in a 'macho' organisation or to challenge the boss on a decision or issue. The more sensitive the issue the more difficult it is to discuss, yet someone must bring it out into the open in order to convert the negative energy it is creating into positive energy. Therefore the more difficult the issue, often the greater the gain.

To discuss openly issues which are sensitive it is necessary for leaders to understand the cultural dimensions of their organisation and the underlying assumptions which drive behaviour, and to determine how things get done. This area of current reality is critical and difficult to dig into. It includes things like the nature and distribution of real power, the sources and reserves of energy and what triggers or stifles them, and the type of relationships which exist between peers and hierarchical superiors and subordinates. Working with the discomfort, encouraging people to explore areas which are difficult and sensitive is a critical leadership role.

Marion Brown, Group Customer Care Manager of Norwich Union, frequently encouraged members of her team to be frank and honest in their feedback about her management style. Newer members of the team were often surprised by the candid way in which more established members spoke to Marion, and by her willingness to listen to and reflect on their comments without seeking to defend or justify her actions.

This 'modelling' of openness was contagious and enabled a genuinely open pattern of interaction to develop over time. Many team members found this to be a striking and powerful experience which they took back to other areas of their work.

Challenging assumptions and valuing continuity

The apparent paradox here is valuing the past *and* challenging existing ways of thinking and doing. Indeed, the very fact that the past is acknowledged and valued frees people from their defensiveness, allows them to be more critical and more challenging than they have previously been. Much of the 'code', the patterns of behaviour and the habits which are the invisible fabric of the organisation have developed in the past. There is immense value in this in all organisations. Many people have invested years of their life and huge amounts of energy and dedication in creating the current situation through the past. They feel, at least subconsciously, that they have the right to challenge it, to recreate and reshape it – but that this is not the case for someone with a much lower level of emotional engagement. Someone who feels confident that the past is not being 'rubbished' and destroyed will challenge it more vigorously than anyone else, because they want to create a new, successful future.

While being personally supportive, the approach to change needs to challenge thinking, and not allow things 'to be swept under the carpet'. The way in which people 'make sense' of things depends on the assumptions they hold about how and why things happen. Some of these assumptions are held subconsciously, unknowingly, therefore to help people challenge or change them it is first necessary to make them aware of them. Often these assumptions are around issues of power, motivation and control. For example, the saying 'if you give people an inch, they will take a mile' indicates a strong assumption about the need to stop people cheating or stealing. In organisations this is lived out in many ways, one of which is extensive bureaucracy. In one company we worked in two signatures were required before a first class stamp could be used instead of a second class stamp.

The language, the words and terms employed, can be used as a window into people's assumptions. If someone talks regularly in terms of 'forcing, fighting, cajoling and driving' they are likely to have very different assumptions about what gets things done from someone who talks of 'encouraging, supporting, enabling and allowing'. The words and expressions are more important than most people are prepared to admit. They can be a powerful vehicle for helping to surface different assumptions in a group.

The leader plays a vital role in achieving the balance of support and challenge, of being forthright and listening. Change is not a smooth process where equal and opposite forces hold things in equilibrium. There will be 'highs' which are wonderfully exciting as breakthroughs are made, new insights achieved and energy created. Equally there will be 'lows' where people feel 'in a pit', even physically sick, where things feel stuck or uncomfortable. It is helpful to remember at these times that progress is made on a cyclical basis. The highs and lows are a normal, indeed essential, part of change.

AN EXTERNAL PERSPECTIVE

Just as leaders need to help people identify patterns and see choices in the internal current reality, so they have a responsibility to raise awareness and understanding of the currently unknown or unseen patterns in the external environment. This external perspective takes two distinct forms. First, finding out how the organisation is perceived from the outside. Customers, suppliers, competitors can provide insights which are missed in a purely internal analysis. Second, helping organisations predict and prepare for new opportunities and threats. Interaction with people outside the organisation creates more opportunities for discovery, more options, more choices for ways forward.

One of the major challenges facing managers is avoiding becoming 'bogged down' in the internal issues of their organisations. Retaining or developing sufficient perspective on the external environment is essential in order to make sense of the internal issues. The saying 'no man is an island' applies to organisations as well as individuals. The survival and growth of an organisation are as dependent on its relationship with the external environment as they are on the people, processes and structures which represent it internally.

The nature of this external perspective should be multi-faceted. An organisation needs regular, direct feedback from its customers and suppliers, it needs ongoing information about competitor activity. Equally, managers need to draw on the diverse and rich experience of life outside work that all the members have, as this can expand the horizons of what is possible and engage people more fully in the process – and it is perhaps the most difficult to achieve. Finally they need to develop as clear a view as possible of how the future of their industry and related industries is evolving. All these views or perspectives on the 'outside' can be described as the organisation understanding the dynamic nature of the wider 'system' in which it is operating. Just as we encourage people to 'see differently' the internal issues, so we encourage them to consider the external environment and the nature of their organisation in relation to it differently. The external environment should be a source of opportunities, challenges and triggers for new ideas and ways of thinking and behaving.

We have talked already of the systemic picture of organisations and management. To build on this biological analogy, if an organisation is considered as a human body it is possible to see how its relationship to the environment is as important as the nature of internal relationships. For example, the human body is extremely sensitive to its environment, and relatively minor shifts in temperature can have a major impact – a rise in temperature causes sweating, followed by colouring. If the temperature continues to rise, eventually blistering and burning will ensue if the body does not move away or isolate itself. The parallel with organisations in this context is the relationship between an organisation and its environment or the wider system – its industry, customers, technology, society etc. How are the antennae working? Are the ears functioning well? How effective is the nervous system at the extremities? Is the nose clear and are the eyes wide open? In our experience most organisations do not use all their faculties, their senses, in relating to their environment, in picking up signals of either threat or opportunity.

Customer, supplier and competitor feedback

Developing exceptionally high-quality relationships with customers can provide an excellent, focused, external perspective. The nature of these relationships also means that they provide a genuine impetus for change. If many members of an organisation have good contact with external customers, then they see directly the pressures customers are feeling and the implications of these for their own organisation. It is both a simple and extremely powerful force in helping change.

John Stanforth, General Manager and Secretary of Norwich Union Insurance Group, believes in the importance of direct customer feedback. Managing Director of Norwich Union's Australian business until 1993, he says of their quality improvement initiative in Australia:

The real shift came, the real energy, when we got staff members listening to external customers, both intermediaries and policy-holders. There was no way they could disagree or distance them-selves from the messages. It was the start of people really picking up ownership for quality and continuous improvement.

This has also been Norwich Union's experience in the UK. Marion Brown, Group Customer Care Manager, explains how focus groups made up of motor insurance customers had a major impact on staff working in the claims area:

Staff were not only surprised by what the customers were saying but also by the fact that they could not predict what customers would say in response to a given prompt, nor could they identify the Norwich Union customers in a sample group.

The focus groups were witnessed 'live' by some staff and relayed by video to others. The staff concerned were then involved in thinking through and working out how to change in order to meet these cus-tomers' expectations more effectively. As a result of this exercise staff saw customers in a new light, empathised with them more and identi-fied with their problems. This was the first step in changing the nature of the relationship. As a consequence of how the staff were treated and involved, they felt that they had some choices, some options. They were energised to follow through on the options which were agreed by management and they felt personally committed to making them work.

Club Med achieves a level and quality of customer feedback which make its competitors envious. In practical terms Club Med gathers cus-tomer feedback systematically through quality questionnaires from GMs (holiday makers). Each year over 250,000 responses are fed into a central processing system, with immediate requirements for corrective action being communicated to the 100+ villages worldwide and trends analysed for future planning and development. Customer letters are all analysed to pick up more significant or subtle points than are shown in the questionnaires. Staff members are regularly debriefed for their feedback, both resort/village staff between seasons and sales staff continuously on a sample basis. Regular round-table discussions are held with GMs during their stay in a village.

Each of these formal mechanisms, however, is considered to be the 'icing on the cake' – the real feedback comes daily and hourly between customers and staff in the holiday villages because of the nature and quality of the relationship. Club Med does not see itself as having customers in the traditional sense. It has members, and it is true to say that if you belong to an organisation you feel part of it and want it to succeed so you make your views known. The difference between customers and staff members is much more than clever semantics, it is a fundamentally different attitude which affects all aspects of Club Med life. The staff members eat, drink and relax with the holiday makers, making the boundary much less formal.

Club Med takes short-term operational decisions on the basis of feedback, either locally received or through the more formal channels which are collected and analysed weekly. It also tracks trends to make strategic decisions. For example, as we discussed earlier it realised from feedback in the early 1990s that the table layout in its restaurants, tables of eight everywhere, was becoming less popular. While appearing to be a fairly small decision to change the layout, this was in fact very significant. One of the core principles of 'the Club' is that holiday makers meet new people. From the Club's inception in 1951, people coming into a restaurant were placed by hostesses at a large table with people they did not know. (The table size was originally determined by the size of compartment, eight seats, on the train that took the first ever Club Med members to the South of France in 1951.) The level and detail of customer feedback allowed the company to take the decision to change the layout in all the villages to one which suited evolving customer taste, and it retained the spirit of the Club in other ways.

Customer-focused measurement

It is sometimes very difficult to get the customer's perspective genuinely heard inside an organisation. Old habits die hard: people are convinced they know what the customer is thinking. A concrete way of ensuring that an external perspective is maintained operationally is to have a performance measurement system which emphasises the interests of the external customer. There is a school of thought which believes that 'what gets measured gets done'. There are two caveats we would like to add to this statement. First, it is very difficult to gauge the effectiveness with which people are sharing and using customer measures; second, it is naïve to ignore the risk of measures being manipulated or distorted.

Having expressed those reserves, it is clear that a number of organisations have taken considerable strides in this direction. Federal Express is a company which believes that customer-based measurement of success is important. One practical way of ensuring that all employees remain clearly focused on the customer is to measure and reward people against key criteria: 30 per cent of managers' performance bonuses depend on their delivering high scores on the service standards for which they are responsible (the rest being determined by how successfully they have managed their people and hit their profit targets). There are eight international service standards which are measured from the customer's perspective. This rule of 'from the customer's perspective' is unremittingly applied. As Gary Roth, Director of Marketing for Europe, says, 'If the house has burned down when the driver gets there to deliver a parcel, we count that as a failed delivery.'

Some organisations are less rigorous in their interpretation of what the customer is saying and feeling. There is a debate currently going on in the UK between train user groups and the train operators as to whether the trains are running to time. British Rail produces statistics to 'prove' that, say, 97 or 99 per cent of trains are 'on time', yet passengers don't share this view. Closer examination shows that British Rail's definition of 'on time' is different from that used by many passengers.

Getting the inside to go out

Another idea to raise the awareness of the 'outside world' is to get employees and managers to go and work in another organisation for a period. Once the privilege of academics, there is a trend towards using secondments in many organisations as a way of broadening experience and challenging some preconceptions. There are potential benefits to the individual concerned and both the sending and receiving organisations. The challenges from fresh eyes are as valuable to the receiving company as are the insights gained by the secondee.

In order to benefit from this type of experience, sponsoring managers have to be aware of the importance of developing an external perspective for their people. All too often short-term operational pressures make such activities appear unattractive. In the long run, however, the benefits far outweigh the costs. As well as the obvious benefits of picking up new ideas and raising awareness of issues outside the organisations, there is a significant benefit in the thinking and behaviour of people who have been through this type of process. They are more likely to challenge traditional habits, be willing to experiment and to retain a view of what is happening outside beyond their period of secondment.

The European Patent Office has developed a programme known as *les stages dans l'industrie*. The patent application examiners go and work in industrial companies for a period of months to broaden their experience and remind them of the challenges which some of their customers are facing. The programme is seen as highly successful and is much appreciated by the people who have been through it.

In ICL managers discovered that when people responsible for assembling equipment in the factory went out to customer sites to get involved in installation, the greater understanding they had of the impact of missing or incorrect pieces of equipment dramatically improved assembly accuracy.

Blurring the boundaries

Some leading industrial companies have been tackling this issue by blurring the boundaries between themselves and the outside world. 'Let the external perspective come straight in and be part of our organisation', is their thinking. Let's not just get better at looking and listening, let's bring the outside in and the inside out. This forces a direct connection, the implications of which cannot be avoided. Some organisations do this proactively, others are forced into it by warning signs or pressures from customers and competitors.

This blurring of boundaries has occurred significantly in the aerospace industry over the past decade. The boundary between supplier and customer has become much more permeable. What emerges is greater clarity for both the supplier and the customer in the relationship. The major aircraft manufacturers have changed the nature of their relationship with their suppliers and the nature of the supplier organisations has changed as a consequence.

When, largely as a result of pressures in its own markets, Boeing decided to reduce the cost, increase the quality and reduce the development time of aircraft simultaneously, it turned to its suppliers for support. The nature of the conversations that ensued were very different from those which had previously taken place. Rather than simply issuing an edict to several suppliers, it worked with them in a practical, 'hands-on' way to help the suppliers achieve exactly the improvements Boeing itself needed. It is easy to see how the systemic view was at work here. The whole system, from raw materials through to finished aircraft, needed to be improved if the scale and variety of changes were to be achieved.

In the case of LA Rumbold Ltd (part of BSG International), a British-based manufacturer of aircraft interior equipment, this meant some fundamental changes in how the company operated. This included having Boeing engineers working with staff in Camberley, UK, to help improve the production processes and setting up Rumbold's own satellite operation at Boeing's main site in Seattle, USA. This clear example of blurring the boundaries has introduced tangible changes in the Rumbold organisation. The introduction of computer-aided design and manufacture was accelerated, effective quality systems were introduced, manufacturing costs were reduced and response time on spare part replacements was brought to a 24-hour service anywhere in the world. Perhaps most importantly, Rumbold's employees feel a genuine sense of pride that their unique design-and-build capability is now operating at a world-class level, securing their future.

The same phenomena has been experienced by many European-based suppliers to Japanese 'transplant' factories in Europe. Nissan Manufacturing has developed extremely close relationships with its suppliers. The company will support development activities with expertise and financial support. These 'partnership' arrangements should not be thought of as 'cosy' or 'comfortable'. They are relationships of mutual benefit to those involved and they are extremely demanding: they require enormous effort and commitment to make them work.

Benchmarking

Like so many management processes benchmarking has become another fad, much used and abused. When done well, benchmarking is a tremendous 'sanity check' on a company's own evaluation of its ability or quality in any area of activity. It is also a wonderful opportunity for genuine learning to take place. Increasingly organisations are recognising the potential of benchmarking as a way of challenging internal assumptions and traditional practices, providing refreshing insights into how an organisation is perceived and what is possible, and gaining some creative stimulus to thinking about change.

A good benchmarking exercise demands that participants understand the context in which the partner company is working, that they explore the assumptions underlying what is being done, that they test the thinking of the managers they are working with. The aim is to produce new insights, fresh understandings. This can produce dramatic leaps in performance and foster a spirit of collaboration and cooperation both inside and outside the organisation.

Strategic external perspective

One of the main principles of our thesis on change is that enormous amounts of energy are created, or more exactly released, when an organisation is able to understand why it is 'stuck': when people can speak openly and honestly with each other about the difficulties they experience, the frustrations they have with other people and what they would like to do differently. This approach should not be taken as excluding the need for as much insight into the future as possible and the development of a shared sense of direction.

Change is normal, but leaders can and should influence the pace, the direction and the shared ownership of changes. To provide some sense of direction, some compass bearing to be working from, an organisation should develop a widely shared understanding of the evolving shape and nature of its environment. This will help foster a collective realisation of the opportunities to be pursued and an enthusiasm to go after them. It is very different from a 'mission statement' or a rigid five year-plan which takes no account of the unpredictability of the future and which probably has very little ownership across the organisation.

Developing this strategic perspective is preoccupying many senior managers. The traditional approach of having 'long-term planners' and 'futurists' has been largely discredited owing to the disconnection between them and the bulk of the organisation. Gary Hamel and CK Prahalad explore the concept of 'foresight' in their book *Competing for the Future*. They talk of the need for companies to have the best possible view of the future, but insist that this foresight needs to be shared and converted into energy around the organisation. The real challenge is to engage large numbers of people in thinking about the external environment and the future in an open, unfettered way.

SEEING CLEARLY

Developing clear-sightedness – the ability to look internally and externally, to recognise the problems and the potential of an organisation, and the opportunities and obstacles in the external environment – is critical for working with change. Developing a shared view of the problems and opportunities is a powerful way of starting to develop energy for change.

Internally this requires a process of open, honest review, a willingness to tackle issues which are uncomfortable or painful, being prepared to challenge existing ways of thinking and doing and valuing what has gone before. It means digging deeper than people have before, not being content with the first definition of issues but pushing on until people feel they are seeing clearly what is and what needs to be done. Often there is an 'aha' moment, when current reality is seen in a new light, when 'the wool is removed from your eyes' and things make sense in some new way.

Externally it requires ongoing objective feedback to complement internal analysis. The 'real world' is brought unremittingly into the organisation, there is no place for hiding behind cosy assumptions, no self-indulgent navel gazing creating rose-tinted views of the organisation's capability. Equally it means looking outwards and forwards to anticipate changes, to identify opportunities and threats and to prepare for the future.

Bringing these two perspectives together, an organisation develops a shared view of what it has to do and what it has the potential to become. If people have been involved in developing it, this shared sense of direction is a powerful motivating force. It inspires people for two reasons:

❖ It is real. It has listened to and taken account of their world, their problems and concerns. It values their efforts and contributions from the past.

❖ At best, it recognises their aspirations and hopes for the future. It provides a collective goal and direction within which individual hopes and aims can be realised. At a minimum, it provides a framework against which people can reflect and decide whether or not their individual aspirations and hopes are incorporated. In itself this is helpful.

Together these create a powerful stimulus for change.

SEEING CLEARLY:
A SOUTH LONDON DOCTORS' PRACTICE

The practice is a partnership of seven doctors, four women and three men, who work with a practice manager, nurses, health visitors (responsible for child health) and reception and office staff. It has responsibility for 'primary health care' – that is acting as the first line of care for patients, undertaking diagnosis, providing treatment and, where necessary, referring people on to more specialist care in hospitals – in an area of South London which is relatively prosperous but does have pockets of deprivation. The partnership has been in existence for 30 years, but the founding partners retired in the late 1980s and early 1990s and most partners are now in their thirties and forties.

At the suggestion of one of the partners, the practice took advantage of the offer of some outside support to stand back and look, for the first time, at how they functioned as a practice and what they could do to improve.

Given the work pressures on doctors and other staff, there was limited time for the review. The outside consultants held half a day of interviews and participated in six meetings with the doctors, each of about two hours. To minimise the impact on workloads, in all but one case the discussions took place at times the doctors had already put aside for their regular meetings.

The partners had a culture of politeness. They avoided conflict and confrontation. People were considerate and reasonable in public but expressed anger and frustration in private. The problems which bothered people were not tackled for fear of offending someone.

Against this background, the exercise had a dramatic effect. The work was in three phases. The first involved bringing to the surface the issues about which people were concerned and coming to some shared sense of what the real problems were. This happened over the course of an initial meeting to set up the project, interviews with all the partners and most staff and two further meetings with partners. Following the interviews, a written summary of key issues was prepared and partners were asked for their reactions. Once some of the partners had begun to say in the meetings very directly and clearly things which they felt strongly about but had not before felt able to say, the pattern was set, others then joined in and there was quickly a lot of candour about the issues the practice faced.

The partners clearly identified a series of practical problems they and their staff faced. People generally felt under considerable stress. Patients were becoming more demanding – and often, it was felt, in an unreasonable way – at the same time as the government was loading extra responsibilities, like health promotion, onto the practice. Long-running problems with some members of staff were not dealt with; there were tensions between different groups, for example between doctors and receptionists over the making of patient appointments. There was a lot of stored-up tension and disagreement between the partners. Doctors operated completely independently and did not take advantage of the opportunity to confer with colleagues on difficult cases. There was also a high standard of care for patients who really were ill, a fierce and widely shared pride in the practice, and a lot of success in coping with administrative changes.

The partners felt that the difficulties were the function of more deep-seated problems. Despite expressions of support for each other, commu-

nications, they argued, were poor. Difficult issues were not dealt with: the path of minimum resistance was chosen which in the long run was bound to lead to more problems. Partners were reluctant to provide a lead or to take responsibility for the practice as a whole: they seemed to be uncomfortable about the idea of leading other partners or giving instructions to staff. The direction of the practice was unclear in some key areas . Older staff looked back to a golden past: they said they felt clearer about where they stood when the founding partners had been in charge.

The second phase of the work began when the partners moved from raising issues, and seeing themselves as the victims of forces beyond their control, to beginning to take more responsibility for shaping the future. This occurred particularly towards the end of the third meeting and accelerated during two further meetings. As the partners spoke and listened to others' perspectives, there were a number of 'aha'' moments in which partners began to see differently the issues confronting them. They also found that there was a lot of common ground between them and this was very energising. As soon as the subject was raised clearly, they saw they had to do more to take responsibility for personnel issues. They could not continue to abdicate these. Two of them for the first time confronted a nurse whose poor performance had been a serious concern. Ironically, they did not have an argument as they had feared. The nurse in question accepted their criticisms and seemed relieved that someone had challenged her.

They saw that it was OK to claim some space for themselves and refuse to let patients come first at every moment of the day and night. They decided to close at lunchtime to give themselves time to catch up on paperwork, and to take on a 'locum' to provide cover for overnight visits to patients. They saw that they had avoided dealing with business and financial issues and had allowed one partner to pick up all these without any recognition. A colleague agreed to support this partner and they agreed collectively to review the main issues (this led later to a change in direction and agreement to becoming a fundholding practice).

They saw the need to look openly at non-clinical workloads which formerly had passed by default to anyone prepared to volunteer, and this resulted in more sharing of administrative and managerial responsibilities. They saw that to want to see patients as 'friends' was to put an enormous burden on themselves and they began to 'let go' of this idea. They shared some of their personal aspirations for work and the practice: this led later to one partner moving on to different work.

The third phase started in the fifth meeting. Partners planned how they would involve members of staff and how they would take forward the work. They agreed that they had only just started: the process of 'straight talking' had to be a continuing one. They held a meeting with all staff to explain what they had been doing and to share some initial conclusions. They were conscious that there were other important issues which they had only just touched on. Most important was the position of the practice manager. She held a central but very difficult role: expected to pick up many of the responsibilities partners avoided but without proper authority or support. The practice manager had been invited to the partners' meetings but was on holiday for two sessions. Immediately after the session with staff there were discussions which clarified her role and expectations.

At the end of the review partners said that it had been a valuable but uncomfortable process. Issues that they had worried about had come out in the open and for people anxious to avoid conflict this had been 'threatening and unsettling'. They also said that the exercise had 'made visible the potential for growth and for something better'. There was a more positive, energised mood around. As one team member said: 'By beginning to talk frankly as partners we started to revolutionise our decision-making process and to feel less stressed.'

6

Working with the Grain

Energy is a central theme in working with change. We have discussed the potential energy which lies untapped in organisations and we have explored how this can be released by developing a shared sense of reality combined with a sense of direction. In this chapter we look at how to work with, how to channel, this energy for change in a constructive way.

The ability to listen, to interpret and to react is fundamental to the approach to working with change we are describing. Leaders in change need to 'work with the grain of change' and they need to be influencing what happens, ensuring that the sense of direction is not lost: steering intention into action. In short they are consciously 'shaping the future', but doing so in a way which is sensitive to the structure, composition and nature of the raw material they are working with. They should be working as a wood carver does, with a sense of intention, some design but with respect for and an understanding of the piece of wood, recognising its strengths, its faults and its potential: knowingly working in a way which achieves startling results for minimal effort.

In many organisations at present people at all levels (including senior managers) feel powerless and exhausted. Yet they do not wish to abandon their efforts to change. The imperative for change – to reduce costs, improve service and quality, whatever it is – seems more urgent than ever. So they wonder: 'How can we get things moving again? How do we inject new energy into the change process?'

For us, the starting assumption is false. It is not a question of 'reenergising', 'reinvigorating' or, as one director put it, 'remarketing' the change process. The effort to supply energy from the top, to 'drive' or 'push through' change, is bound to lead to frustration. Managers need to look to the energy for change which already exists in abundance in most organisations, to work with it, releasing, connecting, channelling the potential. If they can let go of the idea that they need to force change through and instead work with what is already there, they can, paradoxically, achieve much more. In short, they need to work not across the grain but with the grain of change.

But what exactly do we mean by 'working with the grain'? How do you work with the existing energy for change?

―――――――

WORKING WITH CURRENT FRUSTRATIONS

The most obvious source of energy for change in many organisations is the dissatisfaction of staff with the *status quo*. Often we meet staff who are angry at the way they feel they have been treated and the way they perceive the organisation is managed. Many large organisations have a talent for taking in enthusiastic, committed and hopeful people and turning them, unwittingly and over time, into hostile, cynical and hopeless people. One computer company we worked with had great success in attracting bright young graduates. In their early months with the company they were usually very willing, happy to take on new challenges, work hard and provide ideas. Gradually, however, most became worn down by the hierarchical, bureaucratic approach of their managers. Within three years those who could left the company; most of the remainder decided that it 'was just a job', they would do what was necessary to get by but no more.

Often in recent years much of the discontent has been concerned with the processes of change staff feel they have had inflicted on them. 'Programmitis', an endless stream of new initiatives, leaves people angry and frustrated. They have a sense of being imposed on; they believe that those in authority never listen to those who actually do the work. Given the opportunity, they are ready to explode with energy about the way the organisation is run.

In a company which we will call Programmco, working with a group of front-line staff, we mentioned the name of the company's two-year-old, award-winning quality initiative. Immediately from around the room there was a groan of disapproval. 'Don't mention that thing in our presence,' a supervisor said. She told how they felt patronised and insulted by the quality programme. For the staff it had been a con trick: management saying they were going to 'empower' them and give priority to quality when actually all they cared about was output and keeping their positions in the hierarchy. Particularly offensive was a booklet describing the quality programme which used cartoons. 'Who do they think we are?' said staff. 'Are we children as far as they're concerned?'

The challenge is to turn this negative energy to a constructive purpose. Often this is not difficult. What is needed is to hear the discontent, not to judge it or deny it, but accept that it is what others perceive. The simple act of listening, of seeking to understand the nature of the discontent, is enough to begin to shift staff's perception. However, many managements refuse to listen because they fear the dissatisfaction is worse than it is or they do not see it as balanced by many positive views of the organisation. Once they take the risk of listening they are often surprised by the good news which arrives along with the bad.

In the health promotion project we undertook, the first part of interviews with most doctors was taken up with their anger at the way the system was working. Again and again we were told that managers forced doctors and nurses to collect statistics that meant nothing and had little impact on the conduct of staff. They were a bureaucratic nightmare and imposed an additional strain on already overworked and stressed staff. Most doctors were keen to tell us of their sense of being imposed on, of initiatives being forced through without managers listening to the experience of practitioners. Yet once these concerns had been heard, the conversation usually moved on to what doctors and nurses could do to improve the system. Once the complaints had been voiced and understood, and despite a deep-seated sense of anger, doctors were prepared to consider how, at least in some areas, they could improve health promotion.

If people feel their concerns will be addressed, the negative energy represented by the discontent can quickly be released for positive purposes. In NatWest Life staff in one area were very critical of their director. They felt he didn't manage his time properly and didn't give a clear lead to the work of the function. When we began to work with them, they were astonished to find the director responding to feedback from interviews and sitting in a workshop with staff, clearly determined to change the way he managed. There was a rush of energy from staff. From being a passing fad, the change process became real and they were keen to participate. From a feeling of gloom, the atmosphere in the function shifted and staff became much more hopeful and self-confident.

LINKING TO INDIVIDUAL ASPIRATIONS

Positive energy for change also exists in most organisations. Our repeated experience is of people at all levels who passionately want their organisation to succeed, but feel frustrated because they do not see a way in which they can contribute more. In Grundfos we assembled a group of middle managers from a range of functions, people who knew each other informally but had not worked together. There was immediately enormous enthusiasm to work together in this novel way. The managers took great pride in the leading position the company had established in international markets and in the excellence of its products. They valued the way senior managers respected and listened to staff and the investments made in staff education. Coming from the same rural area of Denmark, they identified strongly with the company. Offered the opportunity to work in a new way, they were delighted to give of their best and to experiment with new ways of working.

A key to releasing such positive energy is to legitimise expressions of individual aspiration. In most organisations it is rarely OK to say 'I' or 'we' want. Company policies and objectives, it is assumed, leave no room for individual wants and hopes. Managers feel they should, in working hours, toe the party line, subscribing to beliefs and policies with which they often do not identify. Any attempt to encourage open statements of personal position is seen as too threatening. The whole pack of cards might collapse, it is felt, if people said what they really wanted.

Often these fears have no foundation in reality. We encourage managers and teams to say more openly what they want in order to identify the common ground that exists, and to value differences. People are often pleasantly surprised by the amount of genuine common ground there is. And the process of identifying real common ground can release enormous energy to work together to change.

In one medical practice doctors, at our prompting, took it in turns to say quite openly what they wanted from the practice and what they were prepared to offer to it. It was the first time that the group of partners had done this and some found the exercise difficult. Yet a number made very personal statements, ones which identified sharply the changes that individuals and the group wanted. As a group, for example, they wanted to take more responsibility for the business and management side of the practice. Emotions came tumbling out at the same time as some of the doctors' personal and professional fears. The doctors began to shift their view of their colleagues and of key issues they had been facing. One doctor afterwards described the meetings as 'the most difficult but also the most fruitful' thing the practice had done in several years.

The personal element is key. When a change agenda shifts from generalities and 'management speak' to individual and collective hopes and fears, expressed in people's own words, then it comes alive and has power.

MESSINESS IS OK

Here we come to another point where the approach to change we set out in this book is different from so much of current practice. If the source of energy for change is individual and group wants and needs, and if what is powerful is allowing people to bring more of themselves to work, then change will naturally be a messy and uneven process. Different individuals and groups will have different objectives and will want to move at very different speeds. It is not essential that everyone in an organisation keeps in step for the change process to be effective. Far-reaching processes of change are messy and uneven. People will not march in step. The more managers can let go of ideas of controlling change processes and making them tidy, the happier they will be – and the more effective. The effort to try to order change processes is exhausting and futile. Ultimately it stops change taking place.

In one company we worked with a cross-functional team of senior and middle managers had been assembled to champion the quality improvement process and provide direction. After two years there were successes but there was also much frustration that the process had not had a larger impact on the company. It still seemed that people in many areas were paying lip-service to quality improvement but had not changed in any way their approach to work. The focus of the team's frustration was on those directors who were felt to be 'backsliders': they had provided no lead on the subject in their areas. The team wanted to know how to persuade or cajole the recalcitrant directors into support. Without unanimous backing from the board, they argued, the process could not be effective.

Our answer was to suggest the team let go of the idea that all the directors would be committed. If the team really wanted to make a success of the process, let them demonstrate it. Let them work hard and achieve results in the areas where they did have support and let these successes speak for them. Any attempt to manipulate recalcitrant directors into making statements of support would be seen for what it was – a political smoke screen – and would have little impact on people.

What was actually happening was that the team was using the lack of support from some directors as an excuse for not addressing what they really wanted as a team and what they could do. Before progress could be made the team had to take responsibility itself for its own actions and own success or lack of it. The plea for tidiness, for everyone to march in step, was actually a way of abdicating responsibility, of saying that nothing could be done until impossible conditions were achieved.

Plan – to be flexible!

The fact that change is inevitably messy does not reduce the importance of planning, it changes its purpose and nature. Plans are made in order to prepare, as well as possible, at a particular point in time. The plans should include a sense of direction, some objectives or goals and some milestones as measures of progress. However, they should not be religiously followed, irrespective of what is happening all around. The plans should be responsive to changes, flexible and adaptable to new conditions and circumstances as they arise. Because it is impossible to predict the future it is even more necessary to plan, in order to be more responsive and more flexible!

In the European Patent Office the difficulty of predicting the future is compounded by the nature of its constitution and the control that the national patent offices have over some aspects of its development. The Office has not allowed this to become an excuse for not preparing for the future. On the contrary, it has realised that it can have a significant impact on its destiny by continuing to increase the 'added value' it provides to patent applicants. It is seeking to develop an organisation which is as flexible and responsive as possible, both to changes in customer requirements and to any possible legislative or statutory changes imposed on it.

ENTHUSIASTS AND RESISTORS ARE HELPFUL!

In most organisations there are a range of people with differing degrees of enthusiasm for change of whatever sort, be it the introduction of new working practices in a manufacturing group, the use of new drugs by doctors, the application of new computer technology or a fundamental change in customer relations in a service organisation. This spectrum is represented in Figure 6.1.

We present it here not in order to repeat the often made point that champions of change need to mobilise those who are already sympathetic to change – although this is important – but instead to encourage leaders of change to see people across the spectrum as a potential resource, people from whom they could learn and whose perspective needs to be taken into account. First let's look at how people typically present themselves to those championing change.

There is usually a small group of 'missionaries' who take readily to new ideas. They are quickly convinced of the merits of the new process or product. They become powerful advocates of the change and are active in influencing others. These people lead the way to a second group, the 'believers'. They are interested in the new idea or approach

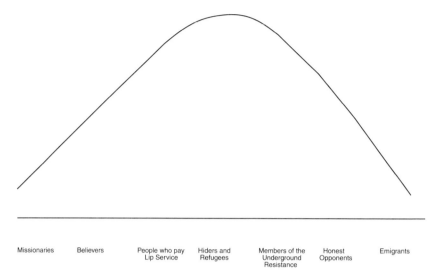

| Missionaries | Believers | People who pay Lip Service | Hiders and Refugees | Members of the Underground Resistance | Honest Opponents | Emigrants |

Figure 6.1 Attitudes to change (from original work by Rehnmann and Harnwall, in Krebsbach Gnath, 1992)

and will 'give it a go'. Able to see the potential, they will accept things but they will not be the first to argue in its favour or for its adoption.

Then there are the people who pay 'lip service', in some ways the most difficult group. They are high on tacit agreement, they know the words the boss wants to hear – but they don't believe any of it! They are difficult to work with because they are hard to find and can have an insidious negative effect on people around them.

Next come the 'hiders and refugees'. They keep a low profile, hoping the new idea will go away, perhaps fall from favour as so many others have. Then there are the 'members of the underground resistance'. They differ from the hiders and refugees in that they are clandestinely seeking to sabotage the efforts to change.

Another important group is the 'honest opponents'. These people are openly opposed to what is being done. Often vociferous and outspoken, they are easily branded as troublemakers. In our opinion these people are usually deeply concerned about their organisation and become staunch allies if they can be brought 'on side'.

Finally there are the 'emigrants'. 'Thank you but no thank you' is their response. As soon as possible they leave the organisation.

The important thing with this model is not to categorise people rigidly, but to recognise that people have different reactions to change and therefore need to be worked with in different ways.

In NatWest Life the process of continuous improvement started with mixed groups of believers and sceptics. One of the first groups that wanted to be involved was – to our surprise – the Accounting Department. There were several managers there who were very keen to improve the way the team worked and the service they offered to others in the company. They offered to be the pilot area for development of the new ways of working. After an initial workshop teams were formed, including customers of the unit, to improve specific services such as the payment of expenses. Staff were initially apprehensive, but once they felt they really did have scope to change operations and decide the way they worked, they became enthusiastic.

Changes in procedures and systems were made and the service improved. Staff learnt about new ways of working: more participative, more demanding, more focused on hearing everyone's ideas and achieving results than in the past. Once the accounting and two other early teams began to achieve results – and staff heard that working on the teams was fun – other areas queued up to be involved. The problem the champions of the process faced then was not persuading people to be involved but holding back the demand so that the necessary training and support could be provided.

Listen to the resistors

Developing the theme of 'working with the grain', it would be easy to assume that the 'resistors' and 'opponents' should be ignored or worked around. As W Edwards Deming said inimitably, replying to a question about whether he would start by working with the cynics or enthusiasts, 'It says in the good book...do not cast your pearls before swine!'

This is not our view. A key part of successful processes of change is listening to those who seem to be 'resistors' and seeking to understand what lies behind their 'resistance'. The danger is that people become labelled 'for' or 'against'. Frequently managers become impatient with 'resistors' and blame them for being awkward, difficult and backward looking. Once pigeon-holed in this way, the 'resistors' become the target of manipulation or coercion. It is vital to avoid the labelling, and see the potential to learn from the 'resistors' and for people to shift in their attitude to proposed changes.

People who are not embracing the desired change are doing so for a reason. This may well be something the champions of change have missed or not fully understood. Just as it is important to listen to and understand complaining customers, taking time to explore why internal 'resistors' are unhappy pays enormous dividends. The change process may be modified and improved as a result. Often the 'resistors' care passionately about the organisation and have tremendous energy if they can come to see proposed changes as desirable. People who don't care don't 'resist': they allow themselves to be carried along.

When people feel that they are being allowed to express themselves on things which they feel are really important, there is great energy for reviewing honestly and thoroughly. Sometimes the most cautious or cynical people can become powerful supporters of change. In HP Bulmer Ltd, a cider maker based in south-west England, the new Chief Executive John Rudgard sought to modify the culture of the company. He wanted to build on the values of tradition and product quality to create a much greater customer focus. To this end a process of raising the awareness and understanding of external and internal customer needs was launched. One participant on the 'pioneer' workshop of the 'Who Cares Wins' initiative was deeply opposed to what she saw as another superficial 'whitewash' where issues would be avoided and participants 'sold a line'. Because of the chief executive's personal involvement in the process and the obvious integrity of what was being done, she subsequently volunteered to be seconded to the initiative full time for 12 months.

Bringing the 'resistors' into the change process is frequently the key to success. People are 'resisting' for a reason: when that reason can be understood and a response to it integrated into the change process, then significant change can occur. Often it is integrating the 'resistor's' perspective into that of those pushing for change which is itself the important shift.

FOCUS ON KEY ISSUES

If you want to achieve a difficult objective, you must focus   your ener-gy on the vital few issues that will really make a difference. This applies just as much to a process of change as to a project or task. Resources and time are bound to be limited. The challenge, of course, is to define what are the vital, few issues. Where do you focus attention?

In selecting the focus, managers face a dilemma. They want to choose issues that are significant across the organisation, where learn-ing cannot be dismissed as unrepresentative of the organisation as a whole. They also want the change process to have some impact, to pro-voke a significant shift in thinking and behaviour. In short, they want to select the issues that are big enough to matter yet small enough to change.

When defining the focus, it is essential to avoid generalised prescrip-tions for change like 'we're doing total quality' or 'we're reengineering our processes', but rather to express the focus in terms which have some bite for people in the organisation and which go to the heart of the change that people want. The critical decision of what to focus on varies widely from one company and organisation to another and needs to shift as the change process evolves.

The focus of the change process in Grundfos has shifted over the years. Initially targeted at making the approach to quality more sys-tematic, it moved to developing the self-management of quality by workers on the shopfloor and, later, to reducing barriers between func-tions in the product development process.

It is important to keep in mind that the lead about where to focus can emerge at many levels in an organisation. Often it is not the chief executive who identifies the area for focus; sometimes not even a senior manager. It can emerge from individuals and teams.

CONNECTING THE ENERGY

There are many different patterns for 'working with the grain'. Organisations have tried:

- ❖ working by 'open invitation' with people across the organisation being encouraged to put in their ideas
- ❖ proceeding by 'organic growth', assembling project teams to learn as they tackle key business issues and act as 'disciples' of new ways of working when they go back to their day-to-day roles
- ❖ working with whole work teams or groups
- ❖ focusing on the business processes which cut across the conventional organisation and working with the people involved in each process

Each has its merits and problems and each can be used successfully.

There is no one best way. Organisations use one or a number or a combination of all these approaches, depending on their circumstances and needs. What is important is that those in authority in an organisation think about how to support and reinforce the change process. This means considering what, and how, they need to learn and what practical support the champions of change need. It also means thinking through how to connect the different teams and parts of the organisation as they change.

The merchant bank Kleinwort Benson realised in the early 1990s that some of its established ways of working were no longer best serving the interests of the bank. Despite an illustrious history and a 'name' of immense value, Kleinwort Benson had experienced difficulties in the late 1980s and early 1990s which had caused it to reflect on the need for change.

MOBILISING THE ENERGY FOR CHANGE

	APPROACH	MAJOR STRENGTH	MAJOR WEAKNESS/ISSUE
	OPEN INVITATION Encourage contributions and suggestions from everyone, particularly those who do the work/have direct customer contact	❖ Can readily tap ideas and energy at all levels ❖ Can signal that people in operations are valued	❖ Need for prompt response to ideas or mechanism for people to take ideas forward themselves ❖ How to provide adequate recognition? ❖ Need for clear boundaries
	ORGANIC GROWTH Bring together teams from across functions and hierarchy to address key business issues	❖ Opportunity to break down hierarchical and functional barriers and learn other perspectives ❖ Learning about corporate perspective ❖ Enthusiasm often generated by working in new way	❖ How to overcome initial apprehensions so that all can contribute fully? ❖ How to sustain enthusiasm and make links with rest of organisation? ❖ How to retain and spread learning once *ad hoc* team dissolved?
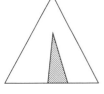	WHOLE TEAM Work team as a whole involved in improvement/development	❖ Teams are tackling real-life issues and context ❖ Learning takes place where it is needed – in the work team	❖ How to provide enough safety so that underlying assumptions and problems are addressed? ❖ How to spread learning beyond initial teams?
	PROCESS Key individuals responsible for business process set about transforming that process	❖ Reflects how work is actually done ❖ If done well, can identify key improvement opportunities	❖ Need to ensure 'big picture' issues are considered and underlying assumptions tackled ❖ How to stay focused on value to customers? ❖ How to involve key actors so that they do not feel imposed on?

115

One of the most important themes being discussed was the need for greater cooperation, even integration between the various divisions in the bank (Treasury, Corporate Finance, Securities, Financing and Investment Banking). There were strong arguments in favour of greater cooperation; and there was some equally strong resistance to that same cooperation.

The executive committee, recognising the somewhat entrenched views of its own members, set up a project team of senior professionals at a level just below the executive committee to explore and review openly the potential benefits and pitfalls of closer interdivisional collaboration. The members of this team were selected for their capability, energy and ability to listen to and influence their peers. They represented all the divisions. From the outset they were determined to model openness and collaboration as a way of working. The message sent to the organisation by how they were working was extremely powerful. While being honest about difficulties, the team was energised by the amount of good news and potential they discovered in the   organisation as a result of the review they undertook.

Secrecy had become almost a password, with rumours creating a picture of non-cooperation worse than reality. As each individual project team member spoke to several of their peers during the review, a 'network' of people became involved and interested in the furthering of cooperation. This provided a vital springboard or 'pump-primed' start when more formal proposals were put forward.

Our colleague Bill Critchley talks of the need to work with both the energy and the authority systems in organisations. It is insufficient just to release and channel energy; the authority system must be taken into account. Where possible the authority system should be supporting new initiatives and providing encouragement. In many cases, however, some members of the authority system are among the last to change, to be persuaded of the value of new ideas. In this case it is important for leaders to provide space for those who wish to experiment to get on and do things. Where possible this should be done without threatening the authority system.

In working with the energy, going with the grain, it is important for people to work both with the principles of what they are doing and with some very practical problems, taking pragmatic steps to get things done. Discussions are typified by an ability to move comfortably between the theoretical and the very practical.

It is also important for people working in change to remember that patience is a virtue. Change never seems to be happening at the required pace, never fast enough. While a sense of urgency is important, it is equally true that when someone is in the middle of a change process it is harder for them to see what is changing than it is for an observer. Checking with others is helpful, as is standing back periodically to review progress. Persistency is a major strength, keeping going, not losing faith.

WORKING WITH THE GRAIN: J&B SCOTLAND

Whisky distillers of international repute, part of IDV (International Distillers and Vintners), J&B Scotland Ltd started a process of significant organisational change in 1989.

As IDV rationalised its production and bottling facilities around Europe in the late 1980s, the opportunity emerged for J&B Scotland to become the main production centre for several of the European-based IDV brands. To achieve this status, which would confirm the continued existence and even growth of the facilities in Strathclyde, a number of changes would have to occur in the way the company worked.

While the distilleries on Speyside would remain solely focused on whisky making, the much larger part of J&B Scotland, the blending, bottling and warehousing operations in Strathclyde, would have to work with vodka, schnapps, rum and other drinks. As well as being a change to a longstanding tradition, this involved significant practical complexities of production planning and management, logistics and overall resource utilisation. Changes to established methods of work were inevitable. The rationalisation process was reinforced by the need for lower costs in an increasingly tough market, as well as the introduction of new products.

The workforce at the time was loyal and long-serving, but traditionally strongly unionised and part of what is known in the local jargon as 'Red Clydeside'.

Having worked out the main goals and major planks of its strategy in 1990, the executive committee spent time together developing a shared understanding of the principles they wished to use to develop the business and work with the required changes.

To begin with, the executive committee decided specifically, despite some reservations about whether the impact of their activities would reach a broad enough audience within the company, not to launch a 'change process' or company-wide training and communications exercise. Instead, they chose to focus on a number of specific issues critical to the corporate strategy. These included developing a partnership relationship with selected customers and suppliers, achieving ISO 9000 accreditation, reducing changeover times on bottling lines, and removing quality inspectors on the lines to have operators checking the quality of their own work. These initial issues were complemented by others which emerged over the next few years as the major changes took place. This focus on tangible issues allowed them to concentrate effort and resources, and approach the broader aspects of the way of working together, flexibility and self-responsibility in a pragmatic way.

The executive committee met over a four- to five-month period discussing how to progress the changes. Recognising the need both for senior management support and ownership lower in the organisation, they established a steering group consisting of three directors and three other people from around the organisation who had expressed interest and enthusiasm for getting involved.

A project team was then established to concentrate on each of the key focus issues outlined above. Each team had two representatives from the overall steering group and four or five other members. The steering group members in each project team had specific responsibilities. One of them was the team leader, accountable for the team's delivering the project on time and to specification. Another was the team facilitator with responsibility for ensuring that the team worked using the agreed principles of openness, challenge and support, full participation of all members, a problem-solving process, review and that the learning was shared and recorded.

In selecting the project teams, care was taken to include both enthusiasts and one or two known sceptics or resistors. The thinking behind this was to ensure enough energy to get things moving, but to draw out and include the concerns of the resistors early on in order not to 'lose touch with reality', which can occur with a group of missionaries. The balance achieved in the teams led to some uncomfortable but highly productive discussions. It also ensured that the concerns of the majority of people were actively (and publicly) represented. Progress was achieved at different speeds in different teams depending on the nature of the task, the resources available and the degree of complexity which became apparent over time.

The executive group worked hard themselves to adopt the principles they had agreed. They developed the habit of speaking openly and frankly with each other and reviewing each event as soon as it was finished. The value of this was exemplified when at the start of the second day of a two-day workshop with the executive group one of the directors exploded with frustration and anger saying, 'I can't believe how much time we wasted yesterday going round in circles, we know what we have to do, let's get on with it.' This violent challenge, although uncomfortable, was extremely helpful. It drew out a discussion on two significant points. First, he was clear individually that achieving ISO 9000 was the objective, but many of the others saw ISO 9000 as a small part of the overall objective. Secondly, the way in which these projects were to be implemented was different. All the directors knew how to 'command and control' work very well. What they were struggling with (and this director had failed to see) was how to build ownership and enthusiasm for the projects so that the teams would really live a new way of working. The directors themselves learnt a lot from this type of review and straight talk.

J&B Scotland used external resources sparingly and effectively. They developed close links with suppliers, some of whom became involved in projects, they undertook benchmarking activities with various organisations, and they became involved in a number of schemes such as Investors In People and Scottish Vocational Qualifications, which help develop the appropriate skills in people.

Over a period of several years, the habit of reviewing and learning has become ingrained in J&B Scotland. During one executive committee review, the directors were surprised to see just how much was going on and how much had already been achieved. Reviewing can recognise and reward success. It is not necessarily about learning from mistakes and failures.

The initial concern about how to involve everyone in the organisation proved to be less important than originally thought. As the number of projects grew steadily, so more people became involved and affected. The tangible results of the projects were publicised and directly affected many people. Over time, people became involved and influenced without having to 'roll it out'. J&B Scotland became something of a flagship within the overall IDV portfolio of organisations, winning a number of awards for its projects as well as enjoying commercial success.

7

All Change!

A client of ours, who is human resources director of a multinational company, is of the view that people don't really change at all. He says, 'They might temporarily modify their behaviour to fit certain circumstances and conditions, but underneath it all they remain fundamentally the same as before.' He is not alone in holding this view; we have spoken to many people who share it. If we explore this line of thinking a bit further it implies that organisations don't change either. The paradox is that organisations change when individuals change, and individuals have to adjust to changes in organisations.

Organisations are only a gathering together of people! This sometimes gets forgotten as they grow. Somehow as various more tangible edifices such as factories and head offices are constructed, the organisation feels more solid, more permanent than a group of people – but it isn't. Tangible factors may slow a particular grouping's decline or disintegration, but at the end of the day if the people cease to relate to each other, cease to work together in a meaningful and productive way, nothing remains. The offices and factories are sold to other groupings of people.

We believe that individuals do change, indeed they change significantly in their lives and their work. They may not wake up in the morning feeling 'born again' or converted, but over time they 'reframe' the way they see things, they use different mental models to make sense of things, to make decisions and to determine how they behave. This change is what causes organisations to change. Scores of people we have spoken to say, 'If you can help people find the key to release their own potential, to feel more fulfilled, they will change.'

Ian Gibson, Managing Director of Nissan Motor Manufacturing UK, told us that it took him two years to come to terms with some aspects of the Japanese way of working. Two things in particular stood out: being challenged openly by peers and reports; and the way the whole management team took responsibility for the whole business – no one's 'patch' or 'turf' was in any way sacred. He had been a senior manager in the motor industry for many years prior to joining Nissan and had come to expect people to follow his orders, to get on and do things when asked. He explained that in Nissan if someone disagrees or doesn't understand what they are doing, they ask 'why?' This simple approach has fundamental implications. It means that when someone issues an order they have to be extremely clear on what they want to be done: what its purpose is and why that method has been chosen. It also means that fewer mistakes get made – the challenges may well be justified. The right to challenge (indeed the expectation of being challenged) raises the quality of decision making.

The second point was the confidence with which managers entered a debate outside their particular specialism. In most Western companies it is assumed that people:

know their own area: some questioning is expected but at the end of the day it is pretty much 'each to his own'. In Nissan every senior manager is expected to enter fully into discussions on every subject and functional boundaries are much weaker. At first this seems quite threatening as one's 'expertise' is being put into question. After a while it is very gratifying to know that everyone is contributing to the subject you are responsible for and that you are expected to contribute to other areas yourself.

In another company we worked with, one of the sales managers changed his behaviour quite significantly over a three-year period. His starting point was one of disdain and cynicism for the principles being offered in the customer care philosophy. He believed that salespeople were motivated largely by commission, that ambitious targets would drive them on and that once a sale was achieved it was someone else's job to look after the customer. He later became an ardent campaigner for customer care, demonstrating openness, support and teamwork in the way he did his own job.

INDIVIDUALS IN CHANGE – WHAT HINDERS?

The ability to change and to adjust to change is an essential part of life.

However, as we have discussed in the previous chapter, people often find it difficult to change or to adjust to change. They are reluctant to let go of the past and of well-established ways of working. As individuals and in organisations people depend on a degree of pattern, predictability and habit to survive. Despite this most people recognise that some continuing change is inevitable.

A critical question which is at the heart of our view of change is, 'What stops people from changing or makes it difficult for them to adjust to change?' The answers to this question are likely be different for every individual: they will depend on personality, which is dependent on several other factors. However, there are a number of 'generic' reasons, particularly in the context of work, for people being unwilling or unable to change. A key role for people leading in change is to help identify these questions and help people find the answers.

Dependency

Many organisations have developed, sometimes deliberately, cultures of dependency. If you consider organisations as machines and people as 'production units' or components, this is inevitable. A component is expected to do a task and accept an agreed reward for it. The relationship starts and stops there. The 'component' is not expected or encouraged to think, to take initiative, to challenge. In some organisations these actions have been formally discouraged.

Under these circumstances, when faced with change, people's reaction is to defend the *status quo*, to 'dig in', to avoid any change. The prospect of having to take initiative, to take risk and accept responsibility is quite simply terrifying. Sometimes this is explained away as 'fear of change', to which the response should be 'to get a grip' or 'keep a stiff upper lip', as the British would say. The external indications of this fear may disguise what individuals are thinking and feeling. Some people will put up very rational, cogent arguments about why they don't need to change, others become aggressive, others deny that it will affect them at all and pretend (even to themselves) that they can carry on as before.

Individuals need to explore, with help, the nature of their concerns if they are to enable themselves to adjust and change.

Chop, chop, busy, busy

In most Western (particularly British and American) organisations people are obsessed with action. This is in many ways a laudable trait. Impressive in terms of throughput of work and productivity, it can (and often does) create an imbalance in perspective which has significant disadvantages. So wrapped up are people in 'being busy' that thoughtful review is not valued. Breaking this pattern can be difficult because, although people may be deliberately avoiding thinking too deeply, in many cases their 'busyness' is driven by good intentions.

This pattern of behaviour forces or at least encourages the perpetuation of rigid patterns of behaviour. It drives people into repeatedly making the same mistakes, failing to learn. Individuals need to create time and space to think things through and make sense of them when they are going through change. An old joke in the British car industry is about the Japanese taking a month to make a decision the British could make in a day. The Japanese then take a day to implement it while the British are still struggling six months later!

A comment in an international management seminar we were running a couple of years ago highlights this Anglo-Saxon desire for action. Working with subgroups of mixed nationalities we repeatedly found the British and Americans hovering around the flipchart wanting to start putting answers and actions in place. The other European and Asian managers wanted to think more about the context and implications of their discussions. As one French manager said, 'I now understand the British.' Using a shooting metaphor he continued, 'What they do is: load, fire, aim!'

Isolation

If people work extensively in isolation, from their colleagues or the external environment, there is a greater probability that they will find change more difficult to adjust to. There are two primary reasons for this. The first is that they may well be less aware of what is going on outside, so changes may hit them quite suddenly, almost out of the blue. This obviously means they will have had little time to prepare themselves for the consequences, whether of new technology, market changes or shifts in customer expectations. When people are surprised or startled, like animals the first reaction is flight or fight.

The second reason is that interaction with others is an essential part of developing our understanding of ourselves in relation to our environment. If people do not have regular, varied contacts they are likely not to be as sensitive to signals from the environment and therefore will be less able to respond to potential threats and opportunities. Perhaps more importantly, they may have an unrealistic sense of being isolated from the impact of these events.

In the European Patent Office the nature of an examiner's work is extremely isolated. They joke about their monk-like existence, in cells all day! They do not need to have contact with anyone in order to do their jobs, all they need is for documentation to be brought to them. One of the results of this is an unrealistic sense of being protected from changes in European and world industry which could have a major impact on their lives. The essence of their current expertise is under threat. They may be able to migrate successfully to a new expertise, provided that they develop a shared recognition of the danger and of their potential.

Blaming

Dissatisfaction with the *status quo*, the recognition of the need for change, is usually expressed as what 'they' (everyone else) should be doing differently, how they should change, not how 'we' or 'I' should change. This is true of people at all levels: senior managers say the challenge is persuading middle managers or front-line staff to change but assume they themselves already know what to do, and how. Middle managers say the problem is both above and below them. Front-line staff say they're OK; it's management which is the problem.

This habit is often driven by self-doubt and fear. Frequently individuals blame in order to hide some part of themselves they dislike. They do recognise at some level that they have a responsibility for doing something to put things right. Herein lies an opportunity in working with change – to tap into people's self-respect, to help them develop their self-esteem and sense of self-worth.

INDIVIDUALS IN CHANGE – WHAT HELPS?

It is important to stress that what we are talking about is changing behaviour, not changing personality. Psychologists have argued long and hard about whether attitudes drive behaviour or behaviour drives attitudes. The two are inextricably linked, but can and do change over time. People 'see things differently' and behave differently as a consequence. They are less likely to change basic personality traits such as introversion and extroversion.

Whoever else is involved, and there will be others, change starts with the individual themselves. If they do not have any desire to change, to modify themselves, to experiment, to let go of some old habit, of behaviour or attitude, then nothing will change. We all have a different propensity to change, we are more or less conservative, more or less risk averse, more or less stubborn, but unless each individual begins to question themselves they will not change.

Identifying the reasons for change

The critical question for many people is 'Why?' Some people describe it as the 'What's in it for me?' question. We find this interpretation suggests too much of a selfish slant: what can I get that the others can't? The 'why' question, when tackled seriously, can lead to people's real concerns and fears and hopes and aspirations. 'Why change?' can be as basic as survival. People have to want to change, or at least understand very well why they need to change, and believe the reason to be relevant and valid.

Part of the 'why' can be answered through raising people's understanding of external conditions; the changing nature of markets, the need to reduce costs, raise customer expectations, achieve changes in technology etc. At one level people are interested in and accept the logic of these arguments. At the same time they are usually frightened and threatened by them. The fear of loss of status or loss of employment is often not far away from this type of change.

What appears to be a pressing, irrefutable, logical argument to one person may seem unimportant, distant or simply not relevant to another. Senior managers and directors may naturally focus more on the outside world and on the future than do people with day-to-day operational responsibilities. To an extent this is perfectly reasonable. Surely the role of the directors is to be taking a five- or ten-year view of where the business is going, while the operational staff concentrate on delivering quality and satisfaction to today's customers?

One of the challenges facing leaders of organisations in change is to make sure that, while recognising the different roles of different people, the senior managers' world is not disconnected from that of people at an operational level. British Telecom boss Sir Iain Vallance has, well ahead of many competitors in Europe, focused the energy of the company on what is needed to be a successful, long-term player in the global telecommunications industry. This has caused tensions with BT staff whose concerns have, naturally in a period of sharp reductions in employee numbers, been more immediate and local. At times it has seemed that he could have been on a different planet, so different was his world from the one in which staff lived and worked.

Recognising the importance of emotions

Part of the 'why' question is much less rational and logical than the explanation about changing market conditions and environments. Change involves huge amounts of emotion, some positive/happy, some negative/sad and frightened. This emotion cannot be dealt with on a purely logical and rational basis. For example, it is fine explaining to people they are no longer needed – they may recognise the reality of the statement, but it does not help them adjust and adapt to their changed state as unemployed or employed in a reduced function or capacity.

Helping people work with change requires a capability to help them bring to the surface and 'make sense' of their emotions, helping them to understand how they might retain or develop their sense of self-worth and self-esteem in changed circumstances. This is not easy, but it can be very rewarding. For example, in organisations where 'delayering' has taken place some supervisory and junior management staff, who were personally very threatened by and frightened of the loss of status they perceived, have found great reward in 'mentoring' and coaching less experienced staff in a much more 'hands-on', personal way than was allowed under the old, more structured system.

Self-responsibility

One important issue is the responsibility that an individual feels for their own life. In this book we are talking of people in the context of their working lives, but it is not possible to separate 'work' completely from other areas of life. If a person feels 'responsible' for themselves they are capable of adjusting and adapting to new or changed circumstances. Indeed, they are capable of playing a central role in leading change once they accept that circumstances can be influenced and that their life will be what they make of it.

In his book *The Fifth Discipline* Peter Senge introduces the idea of 'personal mastery'. He refers to the need for individuals to 'clarify their own personal missions', to sort out what is really important to them and live their lives accordingly. It is this discipline, he argues, which enables people to achieve the things that matter most deeply to them. By clarifying what they really want and continually learning to see current reality more clearly, people are able to take responsibility for themselves and shape change in the ways that will be most rewarding for them.

In Ashridge Consulting Group the administrative staff have demonstrated their willingness to take responsibilities which extend far beyond their normal jobs. In doing so they have redefined their activities from 'secretarial support' to playing a much fuller part in the consulting business. This includes leading the development and installation of a bespoke computer system, managing client relationships, and contributing to client workshops and meetings as active participants. Some individuals have taken things further and transformed their working lives. Through personal development, including higher education, they have moved completely away from administrative roles into work which would have been deemed 'impossible' for them only a few years ago.

Self-examination

Another important issue is self-questioning or self-examination. Is an individual capable of or keen on putting themselves into question if something goes wrong? Do they seek to learn from mistakes? Do they seek feedback from others, from peers, from reports, from customers, in order to raise their self-awareness? If an individual does this they are likely to be modifying their thinking and behaviour as they digest the results of these interactions.

The willingness to do this is very much a personal matter and depends in part on the individual's self-confidence, but organisations can seek to encourage and develop it. Increasingly, two-way or even '360 degree' feedback (which includes input from peers as well as hierarchical superiors and reports) is being used to stimulate these exchanges. In Federal Express they have adopted a process called Survey Feedback Action to enable managers to understand better their impact on and relationships with their staff.

On a regular basis each team member fills in a questionnaire on how their manager is managing them. The questions are specifically designed to provide feedback on aspects of the relationship between the manager and the team. The questionnaire is processed by central personnel and an average score sent to the manager. He or she then organises a meeting with the team (sometimes with an outside facilitator) to discuss the results. The aim of this meeting is for the whole group to develop a plan for managing things better. Managers' bonuses depend partly on the score they are given by their direct reports. One experienced British manager who discovered this process on joining Federal Express said:

> *I couldn't believe it. I thought they would crucify me – and the first time they did! But the next time was better and now I would find it very difficult to manage without this quality of feedback on how I am doing.*

Interaction

We have found that the level of personal engagement is critical in determining the type of learning and improved self-understanding which take place. The well-known expression 'the more you put into something, the more you get out of it' is particularly true in learning. Comments from managers in several companies we have worked with support the view that 'the more of yourself you put into something the more you will learn about yourself'. It is by genuinely learning about yourself and raising your level of self-awareness that change occurs.

This level of engagement can involve personal risk and is not always comfortable. A manager in a large public sector service company used another common expression, 'the penny dropped', to explain what happened when as part of a review he really did see, after some real self-questioning and feedback, the stifling effect he was having on a group of his peers. It is particularly powerful when an individual sees something about themselves differently. This is the 'aha' moment when 'the light comes on', things fall into place (or out of place), enabling the individual to see differently.

In a components manufacturer, after some straight talking in a review meeting the area manager realised that his firm belief that setting unattainable targets for sales staff as ambitious goals was thoroughly demotivating for large numbers of people. Prior to this his working assumption had been that this was the only way to motivate high achieving, energetic salespeople. When he realised that some of the very best salespeople were both sensitive and insecure, he was able to 'see differently' the concept of how to help them be successful. The effect of this tangible change (changes in the measurement system) was spread more widely than the few people involved in the review session.

Individuals can rarely learn significant things about themselves operating in isolation. This type of learning usually takes place as a result of some interaction with others. As a general rule, learning can only be as good as the 'contact' (the depth and quality of relationship) between individuals in the group. A process of self-disclosure (opening up) and feedback (being told things) is central. Individuals can only do this in a genuine way if they trust and value the other individuals in the group. One of the reasons this happens so infrequently is that most groups (for various reasons) do not function very well and operate at a superficial level. Part of the essence of working with change is to develop relationships which allow people to 'open up' and both give and receive real feedback. It is too easy to go through the motions!

There is, however, a risk in pushing this line of thinking too far, in becoming too self-critical and seeing only the negative aspects of what is going on. This can lead to an undermining of self-belief and confidence over time. To use another example 'close to home', in Ashridge Consulting Group we experienced this phenomenon a few years ago. We, quite rightly, pushed ourselves hard to review in depth what we were doing and to learn from situations where things had not gone well. However, as we sought relentlessly to 'get beneath the surface' of issues and draw things out, so a pattern of going into a downward spiral developed. We knew, as experienced consultants, that genuine learning about ourselves was likely to be uncomfortable: the expression 'no pain, no gain' became a sort of catchword. Unfortunately we seemed to extend the view to 'the greater the pain, the greater the gain'.

We learnt from, among others, managers at Aeroquip that it is pointless to pursue self-criticism to the exclusion of recognising and learning from success. In this case a dose of American 'can do' mentality was a healthy antidote to our self-critical tendencies.

Time

It is one of the oldest sayings but still true: 'time is a great healer'. People can and will change, given time and support – often, however, there is not enough time. Sometimes it is impossible to give people time. Perhaps the firm is going into receivership or being broken up following a takeover. On many occasions more time could be given at the right stages. People need time to adjust, and they need it at their own pace, as far as is practicable. Frequently managers and leaders in change give only themselves the luxury of more time. They know what is going to happen long before anyone else does. Sometimes they mistakenly believe that if they plan every detail, when they share the plan everyone else will agree with it and change accordingly. Human nature doesn't work like that. What leaders in change must remember is that when the plan is shared, those seeing it and hearing about it for the first time are psychologically where the leaders were several months earlier. Why should they be expected to catch up overnight?

John Adams and Sabina Spencer describe this very clearly in their transition curve (see Figure 7.1). The curve represents the stages an individual goes through in any serious change. The horizontal axis is time and the vertical axis is the psychological state of the individual. They say that as people are in the early stages of a transition, going down the left-hand side of the curve, they are still looking backwards. In most organisational transformations the leaders are ahead of everyone. They are over on the right-hand side, looking forwards, by the time they involve the majority of people. Their explanations of a bright future and great opportunities fall on deaf ears because the majority of people are just at the start of the downward slope and will be looking backwards for some time to come. The leaders may have forgotten they also looked backwards for a while and so get impatient and frustrated that people aren't coming with them.

The role of the leaders is to help people through the transition, recognising what helps at each appropriate time.

In Smith and Nephew we worked with the Healthcare Division which had been formed to market and sell all the company products to healthcare professionals in the UK. The new division had been put

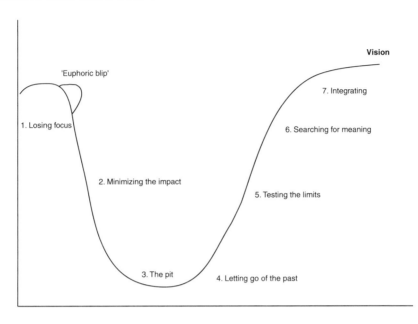

Figure 7.1 The seven stages of transition (John Adams and Sabina Spencer, 1990)

together from three old divisions: Medical, Surgical and Pharmaceutical. In working with the management team on strategy, one of the things that was recognised early on was the need for managers to express their feelings at the winding up of the old divisions. Many managers were angry or upset, for different reasons. Some had helped build a very successful business, part of which had been sold as not core to the group's activities. Some had had a new boss brought in between them and their former boss. Others did not have the functional responsibilities they wanted.

Before the team could start with enthusiasm to develop strategy, managers needed an opportunity to 'let go' of these feelings and come to terms with the new reality. This was done over the course of a two-day workshop. Managers were asked to say how they had felt about the merger. Once the feelings were expressed the atmosphere in the team changed. People became much more involved and constructive. Rational, positive work on shaping strategy became possible.

In reality everyone needs seriously to consider their relationship to the change if a fundamental shift is to occur, over a period of time, in an organisation. Those seeking to influence change should perhaps start by examining themselves and then consider what changes might be appropriate for their organisation or area of responsibility. If they are clear about how they need personally to modify their behaviour or change their way of doing some things, this can send powerful, helpful messages out to others in the organisation.

Therefore the answer to this particular paradox is that by considering themselves individually and changing in some way, leaders are actively enabling and encouraging others to change by example. Added to this, as everyone experiments they learn and develop and become more competent and capable at helping others to do the same.

INDIVIDUALS IN CHANGE: NORWICH UNION

Norwich Union Insurance Group is a British-based insurance company active in both the life and general insurance businesses. Established as a mutual society in 1797, it retains that status today.

It is the third largest insurance company in Great Britain, currently employing over 10,000 people in the UK, with major businesses in Australia, New Zealand, France, Spain, Canada and Ireland.

In 1989 Norwich Union decided to make a concerted effort to improve the quality of its customer service. This decision recognised three major factors:

❖ *good customer service represented a competitive advantage in a largely undifferentiated market*
❖ *Norwich Union's longstanding reputation for personal service and customer care was deteriorating*
❖ *a period of unprecedented turbulence was about to hit the insurance*

*industry through the impact of the developing European market,
changing financial services legislation and rapid developments in
information technology*

*The appointment of Marion Brown as Group Customer Care Manager
sent some clear signals around the organisation. Marion, personally
selected by Group Chief Executive Allan Bridgewater, was an
experienced Norwich Union manager with a reputation for integrity, an
interest in people and a genuine concern for customers. This was
obviously not going to be a 'glitzy', superficial exercise – Norwich Union
was going to improve customer care in the long haul.*

*On her appointment to the position, which was as an internal
consultant, Marion reflected on how to tackle such a vast issue in an
organisation with over 10,000 employees. She recruited, on two-year
secondments, eight line managers to join her as internal consultants. The
eight managers came from across the organisation, bringing different
skills and perspectives as well as different experiences.*

*Demonstrating that everyone is involved in thinking about and
working with change, Marion and her team did not start off by working out what they should 'do' to the rest of the organisation. Rather, they
started by looking at what customer care meant to them, to each other
and to their customers (the rest of the organisation).*

*Seeing teamwork as a fundamental principle in developing customer
care, the consultants put considerable effort into developing those skills
and behaviours which would be appropriate for the rest of the organisation. Under Marion's leadership they worked on their ability to be open
and honest, to give and receive feedback, to take responsibility for
action, to learn from mistakes and to challenge and support each other.*

*Their self-belief and confidence were put to the test in an early
incident of an internal promotional video for use by managers and staff.
The aim of the video was to highlight the importance being attached to
customer care in Norwich Union by raising the profile of the new team.
The video concentrated on the development of the team itself and what
they had learnt from this experience. Unfortunately, most managers in
the organisation were expecting the video to be a more explicit*

explanation of what Norwich Union's approach to customer care was going to be. The feedback about the video was plentiful, some of it quite wounding. The team of consultants came through this phase strengthened and determined to manage their customers' expectations better in the future. It was a powerful lesson for them in learning from mistakes.

From this early incident onwards the team was always keen to take responsibility and to examine and learn from both its successes and mistakes. Its members proved to be powerful role models in many of the behaviours they were encouraging other staff to develop, and their integrity caused their actions to have a real influence on parts of the organisation.

Had they started from the (arrogant) position of 'we are now going to tell you how to improve customer care' they would have been roundly rejected. They were true examples of looking for what to change 'within oneself' before looking to influence others.

As their influence developed they became a respected source of information, of help, of training support and facilitation. As well as facilitating a real improvement in the participation of 'grass roots' staff in key issues of problem solving, responsiveness and self-responsibility for quality, they have been involved in the piloting of some significant change projects such as improving direct customer feedback and developing service standards.

The original team members returned to line management at the end of their secondment greatly enhanced by their two years in the team. A further team has now been through the experience and now, most importantly, each part of this large organisation has taken full ownership and responsibility for the quality of its customer care.

8

Learning While Doing

One of the central themes in 'leaning into the future' is learning: expanding our capacity to do things. This is much more than simply acquiring knowledge: new information may be needed but what is at issue is our ability to use it. As Peter Senge describes it in *The Fifth Discipline*:

> *Taking in information is only distantly related to real learning. It would be nonsensical to say, 'I just read a great book about bicycle riding – I've now learned that.' Through learning we become able to do something we were never able to do...we reperceive the world and our relationship to it.*

Learning in this sense is a thread that runs throughout this book. We have examined the importance of leaders who learn, the value of becoming more aware of current reality and of our own aspirations, the need to explore feelings and emotions as well as logic, the learning that is possible if 'resistors' are listened to, the importance of looking at other organisations in order to learn about your own, the potential for learning if individuals set an example of learning themselves.

In this chapter we want to add one vital theme to this discussion of learning: the need to *integrate* doing and learning. The tendency to see doing and learning as two separate activities is an important block to learning in many groups and organisations. Many managers rarely find time, collectively, to step back and think about what is working and what is not and why. The relentless pressure to be doing takes precedence.

'Learning' is thought of as something that happens on training courses, in the classroom or at seminars and conferences, away from the workplace. Very often large sums of money are spent, a lot of time is invested, but there is a lack of connection with day-to-day work. Interesting ideas and concepts are picked up and then lost because they are not applied back at work.

In one effort to integrate the two activities, we often ask clients towards the end of a meeting, event or project: 'What have you learnt?' It is not always a question that is welcomed: it may get in the way of pressing ahead with the next task. If pursued, it can be very revealing, but many managers simply are not practised at considering the answer. It requires them to change gear, to move from action to reflective mode. It may be easier just to get on with the next meeting.

Learning, in the sense of an increasing capacity to do things, does not take place in the classroom or in a workshop or even on a company 'awayday'. It happens as people *do*, as they interact with others and reflect on their experience. Thus people don't learn to use a computer by reading the manual alone; nor is it (for most people) any good simply to turn on and try using the machine. They learn as they start using the machine and experiment with all its functions at the same time as looking at the manual and reflecting on what has worked and what hasn't. Doing and reflection together enable people to learn.

So it is also for organisations. Learning comes from bringing thinking and doing together. Because people are working on a real-life priority, the reflection has more of a cutting edge to it; and because people are stepping back from time to time to reflect, the quality of the doing can be much greater. The desire to learn, a sense of excitement about it, an enthusiasm for discovery and enquiry – all essential ingredients in learning – are encouraged because people can see how learning is helping them achieve personal and corporate objectives.

We describe first the characteristics of 'learning while doing'. Then we identify the conditions in which it takes place.

CHARACTERISTICS OF 'LEARNING WHILE DOING'

Learning is cyclical

The sort of learning we are describing is much broader than being taught. It cannot be wholly planned and prescribed in advance. The entire scope of what is going to be learnt cannot be known at the outset. There is often an intention to learn certain things, but the learning may be much broader or different from what was anticipated.

The key characteristic of this type of learning is that it is cyclical. It does not happen in a once and for all event. People have the capacity to go on learning, however capable they may be. The process is iterative: people work through a number of contrasting steps from which they learn. As soon as they have completed one cycle, they start on the next cycle in the hope of learning more.

We know from the work of people as diverse as David Kolb and W Edwards Deming that this cyclical process involves a number of simple steps:

- ❖ some activity or experience
- ❖ the review of, reflection on, or thinking about, that activity or experience

❖ the drawing of conclusions from (making new sense of) the reviewing and thinking, leading to

❖ doing something different or doing something differently in the future

Kolb articulated this in his learning styles and cycle work (see Figure 8.1) and Deming in his Plan, Do, Check, Act (PDCA) cycle (Figure 8.2).

These frameworks have been widely used – in particular Deming's PDCA cycle which has been adapted and modified by organisations all over the world. However, they are usually described as problem-solving cycles and seen as helpful tools and techniques for people (usually relatively junior people) to use in a mechanistic way on specific problems. They are not used to help people understand and explore the thinking or assumptions that underlie a problem. The power of the models gets lost as they become pigeon-holed and devalued.

What is required is that these frameworks are used to promote much broader learning: including developing the core competences of organisations, the distinctive bundles of skills and aptitudes which each organisation has and which are the basis of competitive advantage.

The way we like to describe the steps essential to a learning process is: explore, discover, act (see Figure 8.3). It is a very simple version, but it captures the essence of the process. We do not pretend that it is definitive. We encourage teams who want to improve the way they learn to consider the principles and elements involved and draw up their own version of the cycle. Until they have thought through what is involved in learning themselves and used their own words, the cycle does not come alive. This is what a number of our clients, from Elida Gibbs to Aeroquip, have done.

The learning cycle can be long or short. In a matter of a few minutes things can be learnt which are of great significance. Alternatively, a shift can occur over months or years. The cycle is one organisations go through again and again. There is no necessary start or end point: the cycle can be entered anywhere.

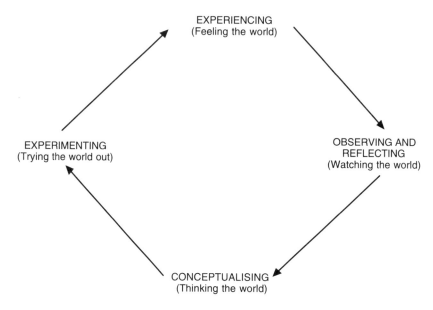

Figure 8.1 Learning cycle based on original work by David Kolb

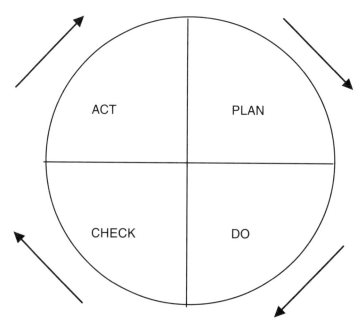

Figure 8.2 A Plan, Do, Check, Act (PDCA) problem-solving cycle, based on original work by Bob Shewart and W Edwards Deming

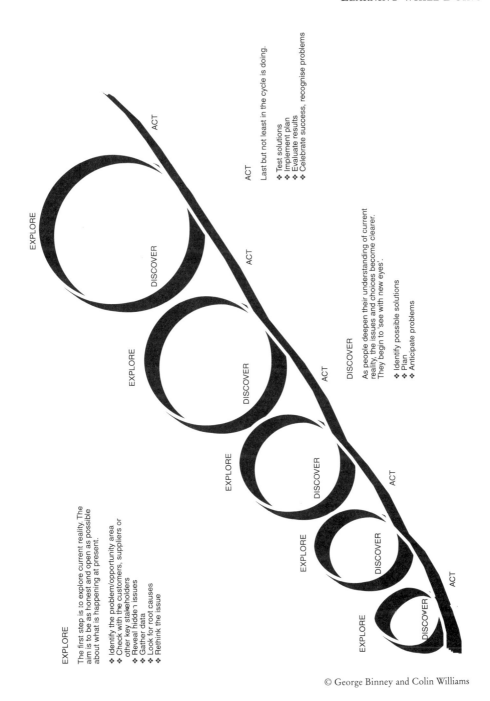

EXPLORE

The first step is to explore current reality. The aim is to be as honest and open as possible about what is happening at present.

❖ Identify the problem/opportunity area
❖ Check with the customers, suppliers or other key stakeholders
❖ Reveal hidden issues
❖ Gather data
❖ Look for root causes
❖ Rethink the issue

DISCOVER

As people deepen their understanding of current reality, the issues and choices become clearer. They begin to 'see with new eyes'.

❖ Identify possible solutions
❖ Plan
❖ Anticipate problems

ACT

Last but not least in the cycle is doing.

❖ Test solutions
❖ Implement plan
❖ Evaluate results
❖ Celebrate success, recognise problems

© George Binney and Colin Williams

Figure 8.3 Learning cycle – explore, discover, act

143

What is important is that each step in the cycle receives time and energy. Very often individuals and teams are comfortable with one or two steps but not with the others. Many managers have a Pavlovian reaction to events. They go straight from stimulus to action, without the intervening stages of exploration and discovery. Others love to reflect but do not give enough attention to doing.

There is a cautionary note to sound here. It is tempting to suggest that the cycle should be the norm. While some individuals and teams do work methodically through a cycle of learning, it is unrealistic to believe that organisations can systematically create this type of experience for everyone. Individuals are different. They learn in different ways, at different speeds and indeed are at different stages of personal development and experience of life. It would be pretentious as well as unrealistic to present a universal model for all.

What the cycle can do is to encourage individuals and teams to think through how they learn and consider how they could improve the way they learn. Would they learn more effectively if they went through all the steps more fully? How can individuals extend their ability to undertake the stages they do little of at present? How can teams get the best from the different learning styles of individuals? How can teams ensure the cycle is completed – and repeated?

A key characteristic of 'learning by doing' is that it involves examining *how* an organisation is working as well as *what* is being achieved. This can represent quite a shift for managers: to focus not just on results but on how those results are achieved and what needs to change in the way work is done and people are managed.

When Flight Refuelling, the world leader in in-flight refuelling systems, decided it needed to adopt more of the continuous improvement ('CI') thinking in its business, it was determined to avoid all-embracing total quality programmes which managers felt had failed in other companies. It wanted a much more pragmatic approach, identifying key business and organisational issues on which teams could focus and learn more about how to make a reality of continuous improvement within their very tough business conditions and tradition of strong 'top-down' management.

A number of teams were set up, each sponsored by a director. One focused on improving due date performance, another on internal communications, another on reducing product cost. Each has had goals and objectives to meet, but each has also periodically reviewed how it is working. The learning from the first wave of teams has been applied in setting up and supporting later teams. There have been surprises. Directors who deliberately had a 'hands-off' approach to the first teams, in the belief that this would encourage the teams to take initiative, found that on some key issues direction was needed. Without clear objectives and boundaries to work within it was very difficult for the teams to take responsibility. Thus managers are learning as they go what is realistic and appropriate in the Flight Refuelling environment with regard to how the CI concepts should be applied.

Interaction

Another characteristic is that this type of learning does not take place in isolation. Interaction with others is a vital part of the process. It is as a result of interaction that things can be seen differently, choices appear and action is supported. And the interaction is most fruitful when people are able to be non-judgemental, entering into dialogue, not dismissing the views of others because they make different assumptions but trying to identify what those assumptions are and learn from them. This is hard: many of us are educated to debate and confront, hoping to learn from the clash of ideas as in politics or the courtroom. To engage in dialogue with others is to let go, at least temporarily, of years of education and conditioning. Yet when the effort is made, it can be a very powerful approach.

In response to the inevitable difficulties involved in communicating regularly between several different countries, Aeroquip's European Industrial Division has developed a way of working which means that those involved genuinely interact with each other, rather than behaving as merely senders or receivers of information.

A clear example of this is in the logistics operation. Gary Jones, a director with responsibility for information services and logistics projects, encourages his managers to challenge him when they disagree with or don't understand what he is asking them to do. This process requires the managers and Gary to develop a interactive relationship which is built on sufficient trust and respect for individuals not to feel personally threatened.

This quality of interaction is particularly important with regard to leading changes in how people feel and behave in their work. As Aeroquip develops an approach to working built on particular principles so this quality of interaction becomes critical. If Gary's managers are to model, to live, to lead by example the principles being embraced, they must feel free to talk and argue with him about them in order to get a real understanding of what is 'behind the words' and take ownership of them personally. This type of interaction is then replicated by those managers and their peers and reports.

'Just-in-time' training and education

Organisations which practise 'learning while doing' educate on a 'just-in-time' basis. They provide ideas, tools and techniques at the point when people can apply them and by applying them really learn. They avoid mass 'sheep dip' training programmes, where everyone learns the same things, irrespective of their current capability, their interest or preparedness to apply the ideas.

Thus Grundfos, when it was moving from inspection to self-management of quality assurance in its plant, trained all workers in a rolling two-year programme, just before they were given responsibility for managing their own quality.

Work teams learning together

If work teams learn together, individual and organisational development can powerfully reinforce one another. There is a strong team effect of shared experience if work groups learn and develop together as they confront the challenges facing them. There is no problem of 'transfer-ability of learning' nor of 'reinsertion' if everyone has has been involved in a particular experience. The importance of team as well as individual performance is emphasised. Once teams get working there is a great release of energy as people begin to believe in the team and in what it can do. When people see the team winning and doing well they also find it is rewarding for individuals.

You can't tell them: they have to discover it for themselves!

People cannot be forced to learn. Whether individuals learn, and how they learn, are subtle processes and experience varies enormously from one individual to the next. Leaders in change cannot prescribe what people will learn; what they can do is help create the circumstances in which people can learn. People have to experience the issues, think them through for themselves, before they will internalise the lessons and act on them in the future.

This is why it's vital, for example, that organisations work out their own definition of the learning cycle. Until teams have wrestled with the cycle, tried applying it and reflecting on what's important, they don't make it their own. It's 'out there', academically interesting, but not appreciated for the significance it actually has.

When thinking about how to foster learning it's worth keeping in mind the saying that:

I hear and I forget
I see and I remember
I do and I understand.

CREATING THE CONDITIONS FOR LEARNING

Describing the characteristics of learning while doing is all very well. How, in practice, do companies provide the conditions in which it will happen?

In most organisations the problem lies not in the methodologies available to help people learn, nor in the (espoused) willingness of the organisation to support learning. Many organisations have said that the speed with which they learn will determine their ability to succeed in the long term. The root of the difficulty lies in the practice rather than the principle. Repeatedly we have seen companies involved in total quality initiatives invest a lot of time and effort in educating their staff in the use of the learning tools and techniques; yet their effective application has been patchy and the issues addressed have often been minor ones. The use of the learning cycle to raise individual levels of awareness, to learn more broadly, to rethink issues and relationships remains elusive. There are other important requirements if learning by doing is to be more of a reality.

Balancing reflection and experimentation

A key issue is making the time for reflection, stepping back from operational preoccupations and looking at what is working, what is not and why. In many companies and organisations time is simply not allowed for reflection. If you are not busy doing, you are thought not to be fulfilling your responsibilities as a manager. Other organisations have found techniques to signal that making time for reflection is not just legitimate but essential. In Aeroquip's European Industrial Division, managers talk about doing a 'PDCA' in meetings, by which they mean not going through the whole cycle but simply taking time out from current tasks to review what's working and what isn't. This can cover a range of broader issues, from how well managers are working together, whether discussions are addressing the key issues, to whether conclusions from previous 'PDCAs' are being applied.

At the same time there is a need for action. Paradoxically some organisations which are choked with activity are learning very little, because they have lots of discussion and analysis but little action to test ideas against reality. Peter Kindersley, founder of the very successful publishing company Dorling Kindersley, comments:

> A lot of companies I deal with seem incapable of making a decision. It doesn't matter if the decision you make is right or wrong. What matters is that you make it and don't waste your company's time. If you make the decision, you begin to distinguish the good from the bad.

For such managers the challenge is to ensure open and honest review of decisions once they have been taken, ensuring that the experimentation is evaluated quickly and objectively.

Tackling uncomfortable issues

As we describe in Chapter 7, fundamental learning is likely to be painful. In changing, people are giving up part of themselves and letting go of ideas and practices that have enabled them to make sense of the world and themselves. If the learning is not uncomfortable, there is probably little real change going on. A colleague of ours has a saying which he uses with people involved in working with a change process: 'It's going to get worse before it gets better!' Change is not a smooth, trouble-free passage from good to excellent. It is a challenging, exciting, turbulent experience. The pain and discomfort need to be planned for and support provided for those going through the changes.

This is as true at the level of groups and organisations as it is of individuals. Chris Argyris of Harvard has written powerfully about the tendency of organisations to want to avoid the bad news. 'In the name of positive thinking...managers often censor what everyone needs to hear and say,' he says. 'For the sake of "morale" and "considerateness", they deprive employees and themselves of the opportunity to take responsibility for their own behaviour by learning to understand it. Because...learning depends on questioning one's own assumptions and behaviour, this apparently benevolent strategy is actually anti-learning.' He adds:

> *this emphasis on being positive...overlooks the critical role that dissatisfaction, low morale, and negative attitudes can play – often should play – in giving an accurate picture of organizational reality, especially with regard to threatening or sensitive issues... It condescendingly assumes that employees can only function in a cheerful world, even if the cheer is false. We make no such assumption about senior executives. We expect leaders to stand up and take their punches like adults..*

Safety and containment

There is one more vital condition: enough safety so that people can begin to tackle these sensitive issues that usually are kept below the surface. Time and again we have seen managers shy away from what they regard as the key issues because of concern for their future position and prospects with the organization.

In one manufacturing group, the chief executive assembled the managing directors of subsidiary companies to meet and examine what they were doing about quality. Over two days of discussions the managing directors were anxious to show that they knew all about quality already and that what could done to improve was already in hand. With their boss and their peers present, the MDs felt a need to perform, to show how marvellous they were. As a result, the two days were wasted. With one exception, participants were not willing to admit to gaps in understanding or performance nor to learn. They were too concerned to 'look good' in the eyes of their boss.

What we often do as consultants is to provide safety, a holding environment in which people feel able to tackle the uncomfortable issues. We do this in a number of ways.

We encourage individuals and teams to hear what others are saying. In many groups people would be more effective if they listened more. Often they talk across each other, they don't build on the contributions of others or show they value them; they are more concerned with what they want to say than with developing the common ground they share with colleagues. Typically managers know the theory of effective teamwork but find it difficult to apply. As outsiders we can help with this.

We encourage dialogue in the sense we used it above – seeing what there is to learn from those individuals disagree with, seeking to look at the assumptions that different people make and seeing what can be learnt from them.

We are non-judgemental and seek to show that we value everyone's contribution. Whatever people's views or feelings, it is OK to express them. We start from the assumption that they have a good reason for whatever they want to say and that there is value in understanding what a person feels strongly about, however much the first instinct may be to disagree with what they are saying.

As well as supporting individuals, we probe and challenge to try to bring the hidden issues out in the open. We attend to what is written on people's faces and in their body language as well as what they say. We often rely on our instincts to identify the key issues.

We encourage individuals to take responsibility, to shift at the appropriate moment from complaining to saying what they can do to be constructive. A key issue here is boundaries: encouraging people to be clear about what they can reasonably take responsibility for and what they cannot. Often people burden themselves with taking on issues and concerns which properly belong to other people; once they see this it's often an enormous relief and they are much readier to tackle the things they can do something about. Boundaries are also needed so that there is a clear sense of what the group can deal with and what is outside its remit. People may need reassurance that personal topics which they do not want raised will not be opened up.

'Letting go' is very important: encouraging people to see what belongs in the past and needs to be left there; to come to terms with current reality, seeing what is 'do-able' and giving up hopes of achieving the idealised or impossible; also letting go of other people's aspirations and being true to their own.

The quality of interaction and learning in a group or organisation can only be as good as the depth and quality of relationships between individuals. We seek to encourage a virtuous circle in which people demonstrate how they value others, are willing to disclose more of themselves and trust increases as a result.

Sometimes we hear managers suggest that an activity completely separate from the work setting – like an outward bound course – is necessary for groups to learn. We disagree. It's perfectly possible to tackle difficult issues in a conventional meeting room, provided there is the necessary sense of safety. Indeed, there is the danger that, if issues are raised in a very artificial environment, they will seem remote from the realities of life at work and the necessary learning will not happen.

If an outsider is used, he or she must also have the skill to help groups find processes for tackling issues once they have been raised. There is nothing worse than opening issues up but then not putting a process in place for handling them.

Our experience is often that the involvement of an outsider can encourage or accelerate the learning needed. However, many organisations clearly want a self-sustaining process in which they are able to provide the necessary safety and containment without outside support.

This is another area where the example of those who want to lead in change is so important. If someone – particularly but not necessarily the boss – shows that they are open to learning and willing to review openly, to seek discovery, then that acts as a powerful example to others. The more of themselves which individuals put into the process the more they will learn about themselves, and the more they do this the more it enables others to open up and learn.

The group managing director of Grundfos spends 20 days each year in workshops with managers from all levels in an open-ended review of the company's core objectives and the reality of recent developments. How well is the company living up to its objectives? Do the objectives need to shift? Does he need to change what he is doing? The time the MD devotes to the activity and his preparedness in the sessions to listen are very important signals about his style of leadership and an encouragement to others to review sensitive questions openly.

The learning habit

Over a period organisations can develop a 'learning habit': they raise the quality and realism of learning in all aspects of their activity. Organisations, in our experience, are learning all the time, enlarging their ability to do things. Sometimes, it is true, the things they learn to do will not help the organisation thrive. The challenge for leaders is to release and develop this capacity for learning and turn it towards those issues that will help the organisation prosper.

MILLIKEN – EVOLVING QUALITY

Milliken is an American company which has won a well-deserved reputation as one of the most serious and successful implementers of total quality. Its story illustrates the theme that 'learning while doing' involves cycles of experimentation and reflection, 'having a go' and standing back to learn.

The company also has operations throughout Europe and in Canada and Japan. It operates in the extremely competitive textile business, an industry in which many producers in the developed world have succumbed to competition from countries with lower labour costs. Its efforts to implement total quality started in 1980 and have since been through four distinct phases.

The first phase was working with Phil Crosby, the leading early exponent of total quality and author of Quality is Free. Roger Milliken, the President of the company, had visited the factories of textile producers in Japan and had been shocked to see old plants producing world-beating levels of quality and productivity. The Japanese secret, he concluded, lay not in ultra-modern equipment but in people and organisation. He set about trying to develop his own magic in Milliken around the world.

Over 200 managers, including Roger Milliken, went to the Crosby College on short courses to learn about quality and prepare to lead the now familiar pattern of quality process. There was a 'cascade' process in which everyone in the company was introduced to the quality ideas and tools. Groups were set up around the company to use total quality ideas to improve quality and service and reduce cost.

After several years the company concluded that the Crosby approach had been useful to get started but that it was too 'introverted'. Too much of the improvement effort had focused on making the organisation work better internally, and not enough on improving the quality and service received by customers. The company turned to Tom Peters for inspiration on how to become more customer oriented. There was an 'independent audit' of customers to understand better what they thought of Milliken and what they really wanted from a textiles producer. It was recognised that getting everyone in the organisation to think about the customer's perspective involved a fundamental change in culture. A series of efforts, such as encouraging fast and frequent feedback from customers on the service and quality they received, was put in place to help bring about this shift in culture.

In the late 1980s the focus changed again. Attention moved to implementing the latest thinking on World Class Manufacturing. In this phase Richard Schonberger was most influential and the company worked hard to implement just-in-time thinking and other elements of 'lean manufacturing'.

In the 1990s Milliken acknowledges the increased influence of Dr Deming from whom, it says, it has learnt much: in particular, the importance of understanding and reducing the variation of processes and his people philosophy, centred on the need to eliminate fear in the workplace in order to allow people to give of their best. As Clive Jeanes, the company's European Managing Director, puts it: 'Most of the battle is to create the environment in which the necessary culture change will take place. The tools and techniques are of secondary importance.'

Efforts now focus on giving all associates the skills and confidence to develop and help improve quality. Pay is related to the skills people have, not output or time in the job. The company's '10/4 goals' from 1989–93 – key measurements where a tenfold improvement was needed in just four years – focused attention on discontinuous change, the dramatic improvements needed to remain competitive in world markets.

At each of the four stages Milliken has implemented with a will and kept in mind the urgency in its business of rapid improvement. It has not 'dabbled' as so many companies have. The results of past improvement efforts have become accepted as part of the way the company operates. It no longer has 'complaints' from customers: these are now considered 'opportunities for improvement – OFIs'. In one business the company gave a prize every quarter to the customer who provided the most 'OFIs', i.e. the one who complained most! Associates receive a response to suggestions for improvement within 72 hours; and they now put in an average of 50 per year. Customers receive continuously improving service.

At the same time, the company has broadened and deepened its understanding of quality. It has changed direction as some issues have been tackled and others have become more urgent. It is more self-sufficient now: it does not follow any particular guru but has its own clear sense of priorities and picks and chooses the thinking and techniques which it decides will be most effective in its context. The company has its own name for the improvement process – 'Pursuit of Excellence'.

Along the way Milliken has stumbled and managers have had to make some painful changes. According to Bob Baird, former Business Manager of the Beech Hill carpet plant: 'In the early days leadership was crucial. There were lots of costs then and few benefits. The fact that IBM was also having difficulties with its Total Quality efforts saved the programme in the early days. We thought: "If they are having problems but persisting, we should also."'

What has the company found most difficult? Two things stand out for Bob Baird: 'Shifting from firefighting to planning more and managing the process more effectively' and 'changing the personal, behavioural style of managers' away from being directive to 'listening to people and to facts'.

9

The Dynamic
Interplay of 'Opposites'

You think because you understand one *you must understand* two,
because one and one makes two. But you must also understand
and.

Sufi saying

Throughout this book we have argued for an approach to change that
is neither structured and 'top down' nor self-organising and 'bottom
up', but instead takes the best of both those approaches and reaches
beyond them.

We drew attention in Chapter 2 to how many top-down change
programmes are not producing the intended effects: instead of transforming organisations as leaders want, the results are often mediocre.
At best the programmes are short-term fixes; at worst they damage the
prospects of organisations making the continual improvements they

need to flourish and be competitive, because they leave people feeling angry, cynical and disillusioned. Many change programmes have a paradoxical effect: intended to 'empower', to spread responsibility more widely, they actually treat people like children. They monitor, control and do the reverse of trusting people to take responsibility.

The problem with change programmes lies not so much in poor implementation as in the assumptions on which they are based. To a remarkable degree these still represent the mechanical view of organisations: change is 'done to' organisations by leaders, who drive through answers they already know. Leaders who work from mechanistic assumptions receive a mechanistic response from those they deal with. If leaders see others as the problem, if they feel that they already know the answer and that their job is to 'push' or 'drive' it through, then it's not surprising they meet 'resistance'. The 'resistance' many leaders complain of is the product of the way they approach radical change: if people are treated as objects to be manipulated or cajoled into change, they will respond in kind.

We argue that the alternative, 'bottom-up' view derived from seeing organisations as living systems – for all the insights it offers – is not the complete answer either. It leaves out intention. Organisations are not just organisms, evolving and adapting as environments change. They are made up of people: thinking, conscious, able to make choices about what they do. Change does often occur without anyone willing it to happen, but people do not get the results they want in this way.

In our view, therefore, neither the mechanical nor the living systems picture is wholly convincing. Rather than adopt one view or the other, what's more interesting is to look at what successful leaders of change actually do, to distil from their experience pointers as to how to work with change in more rewarding ways. Clearly there are a myriad of different approaches and leadership styles, but for us there are some patterns, some themes which are brought together under the heading of 'leaning into the future'.

Intriguingly, successful leaders in change are not opting for the 'top-down' or the 'bottom-up' approaches. They are combining the best of both approaches and embracing the contradictions and tensions between them. They have found a way of leading *and* learning; of providing direction *and* allowing autonomy; of being forthright *and* listening.

──────────

COMPLEMENTARY 'OPPOSITES'

Someone who has addressed this critical issue of working with apparent opposites is Charles Hampden-Turner. In his book *Charting the Corporate Mind*, he describes the 'practical dilemmas' that managers have to deal with. For example, in managing a factory, do they give priority to establishing the excellence of individual workers and machines, or to the coherence, the smooth functioning, of the plant as a whole? Clearly they would like to do both: the practical problem is that by improving individual excellence they disturb the integration of the plant as a whole; by improving the coherence of the plant they may impede individual excellence. Choosing one objective or the other is not attractive: brilliant individuals and no coherence would not be successful, nor would outstanding integration but no individual capability. Resolving the dilemma matters: Hampden-Turner shows that the more successful companies were in combining the qualities of coherence and individual excellence, the more profitable their factories.

It is vital to note that the successful companies did not achieve a compromise between the two objectives: they were not at the mid point. Rather they achieved the maximum position on both scales. They resolved the dilemma, with their success on one objective enabling and supporting their success in achieving the other. The way they managed achieved the outstanding combination: individual excellence *and* plant integration.

This is what we have found in considering change in organisations. What is fascinating is how the apparent opposites interact together. Again and again we have found in practice that success in handling one side of the dilemma enables the other side also to be managed successfully. People have managed one objective in such a way that it helps them tackle the apparently opposite aim.

Thus the forthright, listening leadership we describe combines qualities of determination *and* listening and goes beyond them. The elements of assertive leadership and responsiveness reinforce one another: because an individual is being themselves, sticking out for the things they really believe, they have more capacity to attend to others.

There is a need for drive and determination, of course. No significant change we have seen has been without individuals pushing forward what they wanted, however unpopular or difficult. And by driving for change, at the right time and in the right way, individuals encourage others to give a lead, to push for the change they want.

Similarly, the energy to change does not come from either within or outside the company. It comes from being more aware of the current reality of the organisation *and* the possibilities that are open to it in the light of an awareness of what the outside world is doing. Learning about others helps in learning about self. The more sensitive the organisation is to customers and best practice, the more it can see the options open to it.

It is important to study best practice elsewhere – not in order to copy but to learn about yourself. Greater clarity about the reasons for past success and true current strengths encourages clarity and focus in identifying what needs to change. Changing yourself encourages others to change. Careful planning helps the company to be more flexible and rapid responsiveness aids the realisation of plans.

Those who have a long-term perspective can be the most effective action takers in the short term; those who understand how to obtain short-term results can develop long-term views grounded in reality. Logic and intuition too, at their best, go hand in hand, one reinforcing and making the other more effective.

The dilemmas are connected. The success (or lack of it) that you have in managing one will influence your ability to manage others. For example, success in giving appropriate direction as well as allowing autonomy helps people to be forthright as well as listening. When various dilemmas are considered together, a sequence can emerge, a virtuous circle, in which your ability to handle each dilemma is enhanced by your success in handling others.

The tension between opposites as the basis of change and stability?

There is a larger idea here: that the dynamic interplay between apparent opposites is the basis of change. As Gareth Morgan points out:

Any phenomenon implies and generates its opposite. Day and night, hot and cold, good and evil, life and death, figure and ground, positive and negative are pairs of self-defining opposites. In each case the existence of one side depends on the other. We cannot know what is cold without knowing what is hot. We cannot conceive of day without knowing night. Good defines evil and life defines death. Opposites are intertwined in a state of tension that also defines a state of harmony and wholeness.

The idea has a long history. Taoist philosophy, which originated in ancient China, has long emphasised how nature is characterised by the continuous flux and wholeness shaped by the dynamic interplay between opposites (symbolised by *yin* and *yang*, meaning originally the dark and light sides of a hill). All human life, it argued, is shaped by the cycle of coming and going, growth and decay, everything being in the process of becoming something else.

Many situations could be improved by influencing the relationship between opposing elements – for example, a healthy and tasty diet attempts to reconcile the opposing types of food. The idea has long since been taken up in the West, for example by Hegel, the nineteenth-century German philosopher, who developed the dialectical method, looking at how the tensions between opposites lead to change.

If this view of change is correct, change is cyclical. Always there are tensions between opposites and a constant fluctuations as first one side of the coin is dominant, then the other. This view encourages us to look beyond the tensions and try to understand the logic of a system, the key assumptions that generate those tensions. Once the logic that shapes the tensions is exposed, we have a choice: do we want to change that logic? Tensions there will always be but we can, if we wish, opt to change the underlying logic and thereby the tensions we experience.

TO GIVE UP AND TO GAIN

So we have argued that those who want to lead change in organisations could gain from looking at the assumptions that underlie their approach to change. When they look at those assumptions, they see that they have choices: choices about the nature of leadership, power and control; choices too about what they really want and what they are prepared to give up or let go of, in order to achieve more of what they want.

For some 'leaning into the future' may involve giving up long-held beliefs and practices and may be correspondingly difficult.

What are the things it requires managers to let go of?

Living with ambiguity

Many managers in the West are brought up to see the making of tough choices, and sticking to them, as at the heart of effective management. We are educated to see the need for clarity, tidiness, the removal of contradictions and paradoxes. How difficult it then sometimes is to keep both sides of a dilemma in play and avoid choosing one side or the other!

We remember our own irritation with one company chairman who was always talking about the need to hear opposing perspectives and work through them. In particular, he tolerated a continuing tension between two main board directors, both personally and about policy.

We wanted him to make a clear decision, to come down in favour of one perspective or another, not to procrastinate, as we then saw it.

We now think we were wrong and the chairman was right. What he was doing was holding open issues and working with constructive tension. His instinct was that neither side was right or wrong. Both had good reasons for the case they argued. The company needed both perspectives and both champions, however uncomfortable that might be.

This is not an argument against clarifying what can be clarified. On the contrary, this is essential. It is the case for acknowledging the need to live with some uncertainty and ambiguity.

Abandoning the search for the 'magic bullet'

As consultants we often meet managers searching for the 'magic bullet', the readymade answer that can be plugged into their company and 'hey presto', problems will disappear. While many people are very cynical about 'business process reengineering', 'total quality management', or any other latest fad, many managers continue to look for 'the answer', a company to copy, a programme or a technique to apply. Every conference, every business book contains 'new' ideas from people who are 'ahead of their field'. The subliminal message is clear: if people don't keep up with the 'latest' thinking, they will miss important insights for their organisation and ultimately fall behind in the race for survival. And of course, a legion of consultants feed this desire: 'Yes, we have just the new technique, the new approach that your company needs.'

'Leaning into the future' challenges head-on this frantic quest for the latest new idea. The key issues to be addressed, the path to addressing the issues: both are available inside if people are prepared to dig deeply. The value of looking outside is the light it sheds on what happens inside: the things that are taken for granted, the assumptions that are made that become visible once the different patterns and assumptions in other organisations are examined. The wisdom that is available within organisations never ceases to astound. It goes far beyond anything outside consultants can provide. The challenge is to mine it, to make it available for the benefit of the organisation.

Beyond control

Most managers like to feel in control. They want to know what is happening and why. They are brought up to believe that control is at the heart of good management. They go to great lengths to measure and monitor developments. They want to be sure to have the answers ready whatever question their boss asks them progress in their area of responsibility.

The idea that the changing nature of their organisation is beyond their control is likely to be deeply uncomfortable. Their 'control needs' will not be met.

A more attractive way of looking at those things that are beyond control is to say that managers need due humility about those things they can shape and those that they cannot. Few would be crazy enough to say that they can create the future exactly as they would like. So why not admit more openly those things that can and cannot be controlled?

Letting go of management by fear

Fear is one of those phenomena that rarely dares speak its name. Often senior managers are reluctant to acknowledge the fear that exists in their organisation – even while they are quite happy to threaten with the sack those that are not felt to be cooperating or pulling their weight.

One of the ironies of the massive restructurings that have occurred in Europe and North America in recent years is that they have increased the fear in organisations and thereby often made people more reluctant than before to look openly at changing circumstances and how organisations need to adapt. We see many organisations where fear prevents people saying what they mean and meaning what they say. We see managers shying away from what they recognise as key issues because of concern for what would happen to their future position and prospects if they spoke out openly.

The restructurings and redundancies in many large organisations have worked in that they have saved those companies from financial crisis and given them the chance of a future. But in the end they are short-term fixes. The longer-term challenge remains for many organisations how to improve quality and service and how to retain and develop the people they need. To do this they need willing participants in change, not resentful and fearful employees.

We do not suggest that fear can be eliminated. An organisation that felt completely safe would be well on the way to extinction. Anxiety serves a purpose: to keep people energised and alert to the changing environment. But there is a balance. Our experience is most often of too much insecurity, of organisations where the potential for learning is crippled by people's unwillingness to speak openly. There is little of the free flow of information essential if the organisation is to be responsive.

Giving up power

Managers have power over people and materials. They make the decisions, they 'pull the strings': much of what makes management attractive is this sense of power. Adopting 'leaning into the future' means giving some of this power away. If managers are to involve others, to be genuinely responsive to others' needs and views, they are sharing some of their power. This too may be very uncomfortable.

If 'leaning into the future' may mean giving up these things, what gains does it enable individuals to make?

An end to frustration and exhaustion

'Leaning into the future' suggests an altogether more rewarding role for leaders of change then managing change programmes or presiding over 'bottom-up' initiatives: one that, because it taps some of the natural capacity for development, is more effective and more acceptable to those involved.

Giving away power to become more powerful?

Distributing power more widely in an organisation changes the nature of leadership. Many more people become leaders, picking the accompanying responsibilities. This creates a more energised, motivated organisation. Decision making is done more quickly at a lower level. It is also often done by people who are better informed about the issues and the context.

The need for a control structure and overhead is reduced. Both are still required in a coordination role but, because things get done as and when necessary at the appropriate level, the need for centralisation of information for decision making is greatly reduced. The organisation is much more able to work with and even encourage change. The analogy of a supertanker is often used to describe large organisations. They need a long time to change direction, in fact to change at all. By contrast, a dynamic, 'intelligent' organisation is permanently evolving, adapting, changing, indeed reinventing itself.

The paradox for leaders is that as they give power away, so they become more powerful! Rather than impose their will on others, they work through example and the evident authenticity of their words and actions. Their leadership becomes more compelling and the people with whom they are working are more likely to respond because they feel more responsible, more committed and more fulfilled in their work.

RETHINKING CHANGE

We are conscious that 'leaning into the future' may represent a radical shift of view for some managers. We have no wish to foist our ideas on others, nor to pretend that they are *the* answer to change. There are many different ways of looking at change and which one any individual chooses depends on their values and beliefs.

What we have found intriguing is how many of the ideas we set out in this book are shared by people coming from very different backgrounds and experiences. There is common ground, for example, with complexity theory in our view of the diversity of organisations, everyone unique yet all exhibiting some common patterns. There is overlap with psychotherapy in the attention given to becoming more aware of current reality and the stimulus that provides for change; also in the importance of safety and containment. There are links to organisation development in the understanding of systems and the way they work. There is drawing from the work that has been done on the 'learning organisation'. And, as we noted earlier in this chapter, there is overlap with the understanding that has been developed of dilemmas and working through them.

We do not pretend that 'leaning into the future' is a definitive view of change. There are many unsolved problems in a field that is still poorly understood and surprisingly under-researched. For example, is it reasonable to hope that people should derive more fulfilment from their lives at work, or would it be more realistic to say that most people obtain their livelihood from work organisations and that is enough?

What about the death of organisations: is it better that some of them decline and disappear and allow more room for new ones to grow up? Why is it so common for there to be a gap between the beliefs and values which people in organisations espouse and the ones they act out?

Why are many organisations astonishingly successful in organising the delivery of goods and services while apparently leaving many people within them frustrated and dispirited?

We are interested in the idea that complexity theory as it develops may offer more insight as to why organisations evolve as they do; also in the possible bringing together of psychodynamic understandings of what makes people tick and our views of how organisations work.

We offer 'leaning into the future' not as a unique solution but as one way of understanding change in organisations. It is a perspective that makes sense of our experience and guides the way we go about our work. We hope it helps you too.

References

Preface

page x The results of our research are reported in George Binney (1992) *Making Quality Work: Lessons from Europe's Leading Companies*, The Economist Intelligence Unit, London.

Chapter 2

page 13 Companies holding on to faulty assumptions are described in Andrew Pettigrew (1973) *The Politics of Organisational Decision Making*, Tavistock, London.

pages 13–14 The quotations from John Kotter are taken from John Kotter (1995) 'Leading change: Why transformation efforts fail', *Harvard Business Review*, March–April.

pages 14–15 The quotations from Lord Weinstock, Sir Allen Sheppard and Tony Eccles are taken from Tony Eccles (1994) *Succeeding With Change*, McGraw-Hill, Maidenhead.

page 16 'Eight steps to transforming your organization' are taken from John Kotter (1995) 'Leading change: Why transformation efforts fail', *Harvard Business Review*, March–April.

page 20 The example from the National Health Service is taken from George Binney and Gerhard Wilke with Michael Craft (1995) *Health Promotion in Primary Care: The Acceptance and Shaping of Change*, Jocelyn Chamberlain Unit, St George's Hospital Medical School, London.

pages 25–26 The Chrysler story is reported in *The Economist*, 12th November 1994.

page 26 McKinsey's 7-S model is described in Tom Peters and Robert Waterman (1982) *In Search of Excellence*, Harper & Row, New York.

page 26 'Baking in' talent is discussed in Robert Waterman (1994) *The Frontiers of Excellence*, Nicholas Brealey, London.

page 27   The quality initiatives at ICL and IBM are covered in George Binney (1992) *Making Quality Work: Lessons from Europe's Leading Companies*, The Economist Intelligence Unit, London.

page 28   The CSC Index study is *The State of Reengineering*, 1994.

Chapter 3

page 33   Tom Peters and Robert Waterman (1982) *In Search of Excellence*, Harper & Row, New York.

page 33   Rosabeth Moss Kanter (1983) *The Change Masters*, Routledge, New York.

page 33   Michael Hammer and James Champy (1993) *Reengineering the Corporation*, Nicholas Brealey, London.

page 33   *'The Nanosecond Nineties'*: Tom Peters (1992) *Liberation Management*, Knopf, New York.

page 34   For more on the concept of the 'learning organisation' see Peter Senge (1990) *The Fifth Discipline*, Century Business, London.

page 34   *'the context for designing and managing the change goals'*: Richard Beckhard and Wendy Pritchard (1992) *Changing the Essence*, Jossey-Bass, San Francisco.

page 35   *'paradigm shifts'*: Joel Barker, *Future Edge*.

page 36   The Hammer and Champy quotation is taken from Michael Hammer and James Champy (1993) *Reengineering the Corporation*, Nicholas Brealey, London.

page 38   The limitations of the machine metaphor are discussed in Tom Burns and GM Stalker (1961) *The Management of Innovation*, Tavistock, London.

page 39   For a masterly summary of the different strands of living systems thinking, and further references, see Gareth Morgan (1986) *Images of Organization*, Sage Publications, London. This is also the source of the Heraclitus quotation.

page 41   The quotations from Peter Willats and Barry Morgans are taken from George Binney (1992) *Making Quality Work: Lessons from Europe's Leading Companies*, The Economist Intelligence Unit, London.

page 42   The Mintzberg quotation is from Henry Mintzberg (1994) *The Rise and Fall of Strategic Planning*, Prentice Hall, New York.

pages 42–43   The National Health Service information is given in George Binney and Gerhard Wilke with Michael Craft (1995) *Health Promotion in Primary Care: The Acceptance and Shaping of Change*. Jocelyn Chamberlain Unit, St George's Hospital Medical School, London.

page 45   Leaders' roles in the rewriting of corporate history are discussed in Rosabeth Moss Kanter (1983) *The Change Masters*, Routledge, New York.

page 45   Creating distinctive capabilities is described in John Kay (1993) *The Foundations of Corporate Success*, Oxford University Press.

page 50   *'As Gareth Morgan points out'*: Gareth Morgan (1986) *Images of Organization*, Sage Publications, London.

Chapter 4

pages 58, 59 and 64 The quality initiatives in Club Med, ICL, Nissan and Grundfos are covered in George Binney (1992) *Making Quality Work: Lessons from Europe's Leading Companies*, The Economist Intelligence Unit, London.

page 66 The Hawkins quotation is from Peter Hawkins (1995) *Consult The Wise Fool: Mulla Nasrudin becomes a Management Consultant*, available from Bath Consulting Group.

page 71 The risks of manipulation are discussed in Chris Argyris and Donald A Schon, (1978) *Organizational Learning: A Theory of Action Perspective*, Addison-Wesley. Reading, Mass.

Chapter 5

page 79 The Mintzberg quotation is taken from Henry Mintzberg. (1994) 'The fall and rise of strategic planning', *Harvard Business Review*, Jan–Feb.

pages 90 and 92 The information on Club Med and Federal Express is drawn from George Binney (1992) *Making Quality Work: Lessons from Europe's Leading Companies*, The Economist Intelligence Unit, London.

page 96 The concept of foresight is explored in Gary Hamel and CK Prahalad (1994) *Competing for the Future*, Harvard Business School Press.

pages 98 to 101 This example is drawn from work which George Binney did with Gerhard Wilke, described in their report with Michael Craft (1995) *Health Promotion in Primary Care: The acceptance and shaping of change*, Jocelyn Chamberlain Unit, St George's Hospital Medical School, London.

Chapter 6

page 105 The health promotion project is described in George Binney and Gerhard Wilke with Michael Craft (1995) *Health Promotion in Primary Care: The Acceptance and Shaping of Change*, Jocelyn Chamberlain Unit, St George's Hospital Medical School, London.

page 110 Figure 6.1 is reproduced by permission from Camilla Krebsbach Gnath (1992) *Den Wandel in Unternehmen Steuern, Blick durch die Wirtschaft*, Frankfurt.

page 111 The Deming quotation is from a question and answer session at the British Deming Association Conference, Birmingham, 1992.

Chapter 7

page 129 Personal mastery is explained in Peter Senge (1990) *The Fifth Discipline*, Century Business, London.

page 130 The Federal Express case is covered in George Binney (1992) *Making Quality Work: Lessons from Europe's Leading Companies*, The Economist Intelligence Unit, London.

page 134   Figure 7.1 is reproduced by permission from John Adams and Sabina Spencer (1990) *Life Changes*, Impact Publishers, San Diego, California.

Chapter 8

page 138   The Senge quotation is from Peter Senge (1990) *The Fifth Discipline*, Century Business, London.

page 142   Figure 8.1 is based on W Edwards Deming (1982) *Out of the Crisis*, Masachusetts Institute of Technology, Centre for Advanced Engineering Study. Figure 8.2 is based on David Kolb (1974) *Organizational Psychology: A book of readings*, Prentice-Hall, New Jersey.

page 149   The Kindersley quotation is from an article in *InterCity*, December 1994.

page 150   The quotations from Argyris are taken from Chris Argyris (1994) 'Good communication that blocks learning', *Harvard Business Review*, July–August.

Chapter 9

page 159   Practical dilemmas are discussed in Charles Hampden-Turner (1990) *Charting the Corporate Mind*, Blackwell, Oxford.

page 161   The Morgan quotation is from Gareth Morgan (1986) *Images of Organization*, Sage Publications, London.

Index

Adams, John, 133–4
Aeroquip, 64, 132, 145–6, 148–9
Argyris, Chris, 71–2, 150
Ashridge Consulting Group, 129–30, 132
autocratic leaders, 73
autonomy, 63, 68–70, 72, 73, 159, 160

Baird, Bob, 155, 156
Barker, Joel, 35
benchmarking, 95
Boeing, 94–5
Booker Farming Ltd, 57
bottom-up approach to change, 2, 4–5, 6, 8, 9, 10, 157, 158, 166
British Rail, 82, 92
British Telecom, 128
Brown, Marion, 86, 90, 136
BSG International, 68
Burns, Tom, 38
business process reengineering, 2, 26, 28, 35–6, 38, 85, 163

Champy, James, 33, 36
Chrysler, 25–6
Club Med, 58–9, 90–91
communication, 14, 18, 62, 70

complementary opposites, 7, 8, 10, 51, 52, 56, 63, 67, 69, 70, 157–62
connection to organisation, 57–9
consistency, 61–2
continuous improvement, 2, 35, 41, 82, 144–5
core competences, see distinctive capabilities
credibility, 56–7
Critchley, Bill, 117
Crosby, Philip, 154
culture change, 2, 35

Deming, W Edwards, 111, 140–42, 154
di Landro, Francis, 58
direction, 63, 68, 70, 72, 79, 80, 159, 160
distinctive capabilities, 45, 85, 141

Eaton, Robert, 25
Eccles, Tony, 15
empowerment, 6, 30, 35, 68, 70, 82, 104, 158
energy, 102; see also working with the grain
    negative, 103–105
    positive, 105–107

environment, external, 79–80, 88, 125, 160

European Patent Office, 74–7, 93, 109, 126

facilitating change, 10, 127–35
Federal Express, 92, 130–31
feedback, 89–91, 130, 132
Flight Refuelling, 144–5
foresight, 96
forthright leadership, 63–5, 72, 159, 160
freedom with a framework, 69

gap analysis, 17, 37
GEC, 14
GEC ALSTHOM, 61–2
general practitioners, *see* National Health Service
Gibson, Ian, 122
Grand Metropolitan, 15
Grundfos, 66, 83, 106, 113–14, 146

Hamel, Gary, 96
Hammer, Michael, 33, 36
Hampden-Turner, Charles, 159
Hawkins, Peter, 66
HP Bulmer, 112

IBM, 27, 41, 155
ICL, 27, 64–5, 82, 93
insecurity, 4, 29–30, 164–5
intuition, 49

J&B Scotland, 117–20
Jeanes, Clive, 155
Jones, Gary, 145–6

Kay, John, 45
Kindersley, Peter, 149
Kleinwort Benson, 116

Kolb, David, 140–42
Kotter, John, 13–14, 15–16

LA Rumbold, 94–5
leading, 2, 3, 6, 7, 8–9, 10, 32, 45–6, 52, 54–74, 87, 138, 158, 159, 162, 166
by example, 59–61
leaning into the future, 1, 6, 7, 8, 9, 10, 32, 50, 52, 55, 56, 63, 65, 70–72, 74, 138, 158, 162, 163, 165, 167
learning, 2, 6, 8–9, 30, 32, 34, 50, 52, 56, 65, 82, 84, 131, 138, 159, 160
learning cycles, 141–4, 147, 149
learning organisation, 34
learning while doing, 8, 9, 10, 53, 138–53
characteristics of, 140–47
conditions for, 148–53
listening, 63, 65–7, 71, 72, 159, 160

Marton, Richard, 68
McAllister, Malcolm, 57
McKinsey, 26
mental models, 12–13, 30, 35, 122
messiness of change, 21, 107–109
Michel, Jacques, 74–7
Milliken, 153–6
Milliken, Roger, 154
Mintzberg, Henry, 42, 79
mission, *see* vision
Moller, Finn, 66, 83
Morgan, Gareth, 39, 50, 161
Morgans, Barry, 41
Moss Kanter, Rosabeth, 33, 45

National Health Service, 12, 20, 30, 42–43, 80–81, 82, 84, 98–101, 105, 106
NatWest Life, 11, 105, 111
Nissan, 66, 95, 122
Norwich Union, 69, 86, 89–90, 135–7

obstacles to change, 17, 44
organisations as living systems, 2, 4, 5, 9, 10, 32, 38–50, 51, 52, 89, 158
organisations as machines, 9, 10, 32–8, 50, 51, 73, 124, 158

Palk, David, 27, 64–5, 82
partnerships, 94–5
performance measurement, 92
personal mastery, 129
Peters, Tom, 33, 43, 154
planning change, 3, 15–17, 18, 37, 38, 50, 108, 160
Pommies, Michael, 61–2
power, 73, 165, 166
Prahalad, CK, 96
programmitis, 28–9, 104

quality initiatives, 104, 107; see also total quality management

reengineering, see business process reengineering
reflection, 10, 148–9
reorganisation, 2, 4, 26
resistance to change, 3, 15, 33, 38, 60, 110, 111–13, 158
Roth, Gary, 92
Rudgard, John, 112

Schon, Donald, 71–2
Schonberger, Rochard, 154
secondments, 93
seeing clearly, 8, 9, 10, 53, 78–98
Selland, Howard, 64
Senge, Peter, 129, 138
7-S model, 26
Sheppard, Sir Allen, 15
Shewart, Bob, 142
Smith and Nephew, 133–4

Spencer, Sabina, 133–4
Stalker, GM, 38
Stanforth, John, 89–90

top-down change programmes, 2–3, 4, 6, 8, 9, 10, 13, 157–8, 166
consequences of, 29–30
contribution of, 17–18
problems with, 18–29
total quality management, 2, 27, 144, 153, 155, 163; see also quality initiatives
training, 3, 10, 146
transition curve, 133–4
Trigano, Serge, 58

Vallance, Sir Iain, 128
vision, 2, 3, 10, 13–14, 17, 21–4, 34, 35, 37, 38, 43–4, 45, 60, 78–80, 82

Waterman, Robert, 26, 33
Weinstock, Lord, 14, 15
Wickens, Peter, 59
Willats, Peter, 41
working with the grain, 8, 9, 10, 53, 102–17; see also energy

THE FRONTIERS OF EXCELLENCE

LEARNING FROM
COMPANIES THAT PUT
PEOPLE FIRST

ROBERT WATERMAN

"Very readable . . . with **The Frontiers of Excellence,** *Waterman deserves to hit the same heights as Peters. Valuable insights emerge from the wealth of practical detail."*
Christopher Lorenz, The Financial Times

"The best of America's best, distilled by an expert."
Charles Handy

This new book from the co-author of the all-time business bestseller *In Search Of Excellence* explores the fundamental secrets of success of some of the world's most admired companies. Waterman's purpose is simple; to discover, in depth and at first hand the reason that these organisations (including a school in the Bronx) do so well.

Robert Waterman reveals that firms at the new frontiers of excellence organise around their own people and in ways that meet and anticipate customer needs. Waterman's crisp case studies give us an insider's view of why these firms are so good. It also has other fascinating and surprising insights:

* Companies that set profits as their number one goal are actually <u>less</u> profitable in the long run than people-centred organisations

* Organisation <u>is</u> strategy

Robert Waterman is co-author of *In Search of Excellence* and author of *The Renewal Factor* and *Adhocracy: The Power to Change*. He left McKinsey as a senior director in 1985 to form the Waterman Group, Inc.

£16.99 HB 1 85788 040 4
£9.99 PB 1 85788 081 1
320pp 234x156mm

THE FIFTH DISCIPLINE FIELDBOOK

STRATEGIES AND TOOLS FOR BUILDING
A LEARNING ORGANISATION

PETER SENGE,

ART KLEINER, CHARLOTTE ROBERTS,
RICHARD ROSS, BRYAN SMITH

"The Fieldbook will become the most referenced, quoted and used business book of the 1990s. If you can afford only one book to help you achieve organisational change, this is the book."
Herb Rau, Total Quality Manager, National Semiconductor

Peter Senge's international bestseller, *The Fifth Discipline*, revolutionised the practice of management by introducing the theory of learning organisations. Now Dr. Senge moves from the philosophical to the practical by answering the first question all lovers of the learning organisation ask: What do they do on Monday morning?

The Fieldbook is an intensely pragmatic guide. It shows how to create an organisation of learners where memories are brought to life, where collaboration is the life-blood of every endeavour, and where tough questions are fearlessly asked. The stories in this book show that businesses, schools, agencies and even communities can undo their 'learning disabilities' and achieve superior performance. If ever a book gave meaning to the phrase 'hands-on', this is it.

You don't have to have read *The Fifth Discipline* to understand *The Fieldbook*, which contains summaries of Senge's key theoretical ideas. This is a book which will have you creating a learning organisation from the very first chapter!

Peter Senge is the Director of the Center for Organizational Learning at MIT's Sloan School of Management, and a founding partner of Innovation Associates in Boston.

£19.99 Softback 1 85788 060 9
608pp 230x186mm
with gatefold flaps

MANAGING TRANSITIONS

MAKING THE MOST OF CHANGE

WILLIAM BRIDGES

Everybody talks about "managing change" but this US bestseller provides both a real sense of the emotional impact of change and clear, specific guidelines for both people and organisations to successfully navigate change.

"Change and rate of change are more dynamic today than ever. Bill Bridges has attacked an area of managing change that many not only avoid, but also not even recognise - the human side of change. Managing Transitions *can certainly help an organisation understand change better and develop improved change strategies. This is a valuable contribution."*

Robert Levy, Personnel Manager, Hewlett-Packard Company

"Bill Bridges is right on target. The situational examples are very real-to-life - Managing Transitions *is exactly right for corporate employees. It's one of the best books I've read."*

Debbie Biondolillo, VP Human Resources, Apple Computer

Directed at managers and employees in today's corporations, where change is necessary to revitalize and improve corporate performance, *Managing Transitions* addresses the fact that it is *people* that have to carry out the change. It not only talks about what should be done, but also shows how to do it, giving managers practical ways to bring everybody "on board".

Whenever an organisation makes a change, its people have to deal with, first, an ending; then with a time in between the old and the new that Bridges calls "the neutral zone"; and then with a new beginning. William Bridges is the first to talk about what is going on inside the people who have to make the change work; and the first to provide any real sense of the emotional impact of change and what can be done to keep it from disrupting the entire organization.

William Bridges, PhD, is a consultant and lecturer based in Mill Valley, California. He is the author of the bestseller *Jobshift: How to Prosper in a Workplace Without Jobs* (Nicholas Brealey) and the classic *Transitions*, read by more than a quarter of a million people. Formerly a Professor of English, he made a shift to the field of transition management in the mid 1970s. *The Wall Street Journal* listed him in 1993 among the ten most popular executive development consultants in the US.

£9.99 PB 1 85788 112 5
140pp 234x189mm

ORDER FORM

Titles are available from all good bookshops, OR

SEND YOUR COMPLETED ORDER TO:

Nicholas Brealey Publishing

36 John Street
London
WC1N 2AT, UK
Tel: +44 (0)171 430 0224
Fax: +44 (0)171 404 8311

17470 Sonoma Highway
Sonoma
California 95476, USA
Tel: (707) 939 7570
Fax: (707) 938 3515

Title	ISBN	Price	Qty	Cost
			Sub-total	
Postage (UK or surface mail outside the UK)				+ £2.95
OR Postage Airmail (add £8.00 and delete £2.95 above)				
			TOTAL	

BY CHEQUE:

I enclose a cheque (payable to Nicholas Brealey Publishing) for £ . . . .

BY CREDIT CARD:

I authorise you to debit my credit card account for £ . . . .
My Access/Visa/American Express/Diners Club card number is:

Expiry date: . . . . .Tel no: . . . .

Cardholder's Name: . . . . .Signature: . . . .

Position: . . . . .Organisation: . . . .

Address: . . . . .Postcode: . . . .

Pro Forma Invoices issued on request: Please tick   ☐

Bulk Order discounts are available.

If you do not wish to receive further information please tick this box   ☐